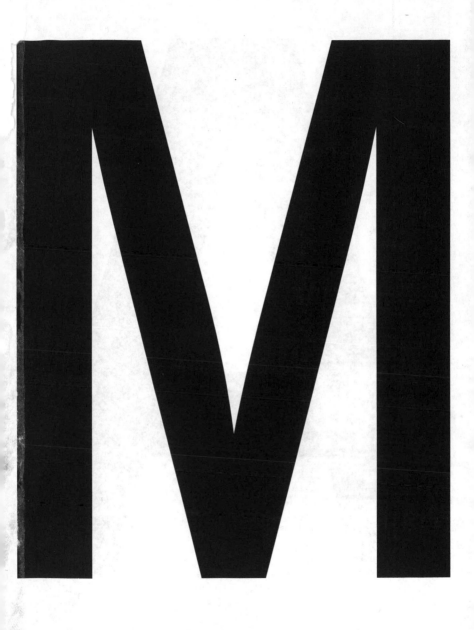

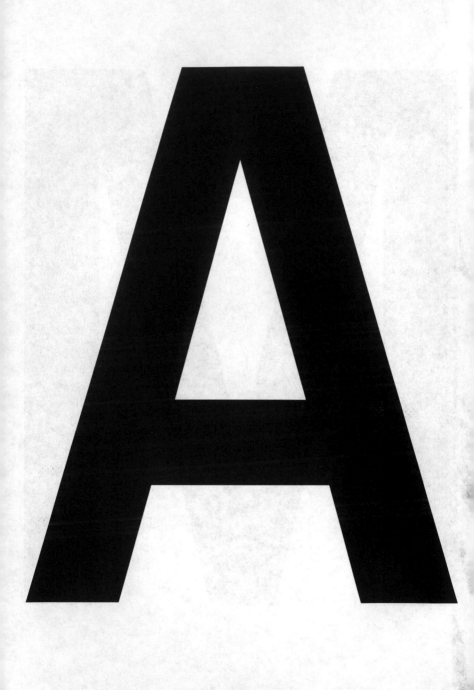

Books by David Ogilvy

OGILVY ON ADVERTISING (1983)
BLOOD, BRAINS and BEER: An Autobiography (1978)

Confessions of an Advertising Man

David Ogilvy

southbank
publishing

This edition published 2004

Reprinted 2005, 2006

Southbank Publishing
21 Great Ormond Street
London WC1N 3JB

www.southbankpublishing.com

A CIP catalogue record for this book is available from the
British Library.

ISBN 10: 1 904915 01 9
ISBN 13: 978 1 904915 01 0

4 6 8 10 9 7 5 3

Typeset by Avocet Typeset, Chilton, Aylesbury, Bucks
Printed by CPD, Ebbw Vale, Wales

David Ogilvy

DAVID OGILVY was born in 1911 in West Horsley, England. Educated at Fettes College, Edinburgh, and Christ Church, Oxford, he started his career as an apprentice chef in the kitchens of the Hotel Majestic in Paris. He went on from Paris to sell stoves in Scotland, and later emigrated to America to become Associate Director of Dr. George Gallup's Audience Research Institute at Princeton.

During the Second World War, Mr. Ogilvy was on Sir William Stephenson's staff in British Security Coordination. After the war, he founded the advertising agency known today as Ogilvy and Mather.

Contents

Foreword 11

The Story Behind This Book 15

Background 29

I How to Manage an Advertising Agency 33

II How to Get Clients 51

III How to Keep Clients 84

IV How to Be a Good Client 100

V How to Build Great Campaigns 117

VI How to Write Potent Copy 133

VII How to Illustrate Advertisements and Posters 144

VIII How to Make Good Television Commercials 159

IX How to Make Good Campaigns for Food Products, Tourist Destinations and Proprietary Medicines 164

X How to Rise to the Top of the Tree – Advice to the Young 171

XI Should Advertising Be Abolished? 179

Index 197

Foreword

I first read this seminal book as a junior copywriter in the mid-Sixties. One of my first bosses was Peter Mayle (who went on to write some very successful books of his own). Peter had recently arrived in London from Ogilvy's in New York and consequently *Confessions of an Advertising Man,* published in 1963, was required reading for all of us young turks, in our button-down shirts and thick welted shoes, who were brown-nosing our way to the best assignments. Ogilvy's slender but juicy book was easy to read and eminently quotable as we spouted his words of wisdom in the elevators and toilets. To say it was our bible might draw Ogilvy's opprobrium for 'vacuous exhortations,' but it certainly was the equivalent of the Little Red Book of Mao for my Sixties ad generation earnestly searching for what Ogilvy called "the ticket on the meat."

We particularly liked the line, "When people aren't having any fun, they seldom produce good work." Peter Mayle, our interpreter of "the good book according to Ogilvy," said that this meant "the mavericks" – the creative people – should indulge in long lunches in Soho. Indeed, one rarely repeated heretical Ogilvy nugget stated that, "People are more productive when they drink. I find if I drink two or three brandies, I am better able to write." This of course became the mantra for an entire generation of advertising folk as we became better paid, along with the Sixties explosion, and traded in our Cortinas for snazzier models. After all, "Pay people peanuts and you get monkeys," said Ogilvy. We loved that one.

I suspect that Ogilvy's Turnbull & Asser shirts and puffing pipe were as much an egregious concoction as the man in the Hathaway eye patch he had made famous, but who could fail to be seduced by a little British narcissism fused with hard-nosed American, self-serving salesmanship.

Famously stating that "ninety-nine percent of advertising doesn't sell much of anything to anyone," it's easy to see how this book became such required reading when it was first published. Quoting everyone from Mencken to Churchill; from Savignac to Mikoyan; from P.T. Barnum to Aldous Huxley, Ogilvy, the (briefly) Oxford-educated Madison Avenue honcho, made advertising not only cool but also, for the first time, almost respectable.

Anecdotal, aphoristic and oozing with self-confidence, the pages of *Confessions* are packed with Ogilvy 'commandments' as he offers advice to everyone in advertising from the mailroom, to the clients. His own Hemingway-esque personal history – Paris chef to Amish farmer – was possibly as richly embellished as Commander Whitehead's at Schweppes. He never lacked for self-esteem and his faith in his agency was absolute, as he talked-up himself and, consequently, the firm that bore his name: Ogilvy, Benson & Mather. (Note there's no possibility of democratic alphabetical order with wily David.)

Looking back after four decades, his own ads probably look a little dusty, which is to be expected, but his broader ideas still fit the world in which we live today. Many of his oft-repeated words have become truisms in a more cynical age: Leaders grasp nettles; Don't keep a dog and bark yourself; Hire people who are better than you are; You can't save souls in an empty church . . .

Ultimately, this book is important because it's not just about advertising, it's also about how people think and behave at the sharp end of business – any business. In fact, one of the better known quotes isn't specifically about advertising at all: "I admire people with gentle manners, who treat other people as human beings. I abhor quarrelsome people who wage paper warfare . . . I despise toadies who suck up to their bosses; they are generally the same people who bully their subordinates."

As an Englishman interested in baseball, Ogilvy says: "Don't bunt. Aim out of the park. Aim for the company of immortals."

In the world of advertising, this little book has ensured him that company.

Sir Alan Parker

The Story Behind This Book

Fourteen years before writing these *Confessions*, I had gone to New York and started an advertising agency. Americans thought I was crazy. What could a Scotsman know about advertising?

My agency was an *immediate* and *meteoric* success.

I wrote this book during my summer vacation in 1962, and gave the copyright to my son for his twenty-first birthday. I thought it would sell 4,000 copies. To my surprise, it was a runaway best seller, and was later translated into fourteen languages. So far, about a million copies have been sold.

Why did I write it? *First,* to attract new clients to my advertising agency. *Second,* to condition the market for a public offering of our shares. *Third,* to make myself better known in the business world. It achieved all three of these purposes.

If I were writing it today, it would he less indiscreet, less boastful, and less didactic. You will find that it is full of *rules* – do this, do that, don't do the other thing. Advertising people, particularly young ones, are allergic to rules. Today I would not say, "Never set copy in reverse." I would say, "Research shows that when you set copy in reverse, nobody will read it." A more tactful formula in our permissive society.

My colleagues at Ogilvy & Mather have largely followed my precepts, and they have sold a lot of products for a lot of manu-facturers, with the result that our agency is now sixty times as big as it was when I wrote this book. Instead of one office and nineteen clients, we now have three thousand clients and 267 offices including 44 in the United States.

I get letters from strangers who thank me for the dramatic improvement in their sales when they follow the advice contained in this book. And I meet big shots in the world of marketing who say that they owe their careers to reading my *Confessions* when they were starting out.

I apologize for referring to the people who work in advertising as *men*. Please remember that I was writing twenty-five years ago, when the large majority were *men*. Today the large majority are *women*. Thank heaven.

If you detect a slight stench of conceit in this book, I would have you know that my conceit is selective. I am a miserable duffer in everything *except* advertising. I cannot read a balance sheet, work a computer, ski, sail, play golf, or paint. But when it comes to advertising, *Advertising Age* says that I am "the creative King of advertising." When *Fortune* published an article about me and titled it: "is David Ogilvy a Genius?," I asked my lawyer to sue the editor for the question mark.

Not long afterward, I became an extinct volcano and took refuge in "management." But I got fed up with the hurly-burly on Madison Avenue and went to live in the middle of France, where I garden – and bombard my partners with busybody memos.

Generally speaking, my precepts – most of them based on research – are as valid today as they were in 1962. But *Confessions* contains three statements which need correction:

On page 154, I wrote that "when your advertisement is to contain a coupon and you want the maximum returns, put it at the top, bang in the middle." This isn't true today. Put your coupon *bottom right.*

On page 159, I wrote that "there is no correlation between people *liking* commercials and being *sold* by them." Recent research at the Ogilvy Center for Research and Development has revealed that commercials which people like sell more than commercials they don't like.

On page 160, I advised the reader to restrict himself to ninety words a minute in television commercials. It is now known that, on average, 200 words a minute sells more of your product. Pitchmen in open-air markets know this, so they talk fast.

Chapter 8 on television commercials is inadequate. I can only plead that, in 1962, very little was known about what works and what doesn't work on television. You can find some later research in my book *Ogilvy on Advertising*, published by Crown in 1983.

Confessions says nothing about corporate culture, notably the corporate culture of advertising agencies. In 1962 I had never heard of corporate culture, nor had anybody else. Thanks to two students of business, Terence Deal and Allen Kennedy, we now know that "the people who built the companies for which America is famous, all worked obsessively *to create strong cultures within their organizations*. Companies that have cultivated their individual identities by shaping values, making heroes, spelling out rites and rituals, and acknowledging the cultural network have an edge."

Now the concept of corporate culture has caught on in a big way, not only in the United States, but also in England. Frances Cairneross of *The Economist* has written: 'The common characteristic of success is the deliberate creation of a corporate culture."

The head of one of the biggest agencies recently told me, "Ogilvy & Mather is the only agency in the world with a real corporate culture." It may be this, more than anything else, which differentiates us from our competitors. Here is how I see our culture:

Some of our people spend their entire working lives in our agency. We do our damnedest to make it a nice place to work. We put this first.

We treat our people like human beings. We help them when they are in trouble-with their jobs, with illness, with alcoholism, and so on.

We help them make the best of their talents, investing an awful lot of time and money in training-like a teaching hospital.

Our system of management is singularly democratic. We don't like hierarchical bureaucracy or rigid pecking orders.

We give our executives an extraordinary degree of freedom and independence.

We like people with gentle manners. Our New York office gives an annual award for "professionalism combined with *civility*."

We like people who are honest in argument, honest with clients and, above all, honest with consumers.

We admire people who work hard, who are objective and thorough.

We detest office politicians, toadies, bullies, and pompous asses. We abhor ruthlessness.

The way up our ladder is open to everybody. We are free from prejudice of any kind – religious prejudice, racial prejudice, or sexual prejudice.

We detest nepotism and every other form of favoritism. In promoting people to top jobs, we are influenced as much by their *character* as anything else.

The recommendations we make to our clients are the recommendations we would make if we owned their companies, without regard to our own interest.

What most clients want from agencies is good advertising campaigns. We put the creative function at the top of our priorities.

The line between pride in our work and neurotic obstinacy is a narrow one. We do not grudge our clients the right to decide what advertising to run. It is their money.

Many of our clients employ us in several countries. It is important for them to know that they can expect the same standards of behavior in all our offices. That is why we want our culture to be the same all over the world.

We try to sell our clients' products without offending the *mores* of the countries where we do business.

We attach importance to *discretion*. Clients don't appreciate agencies which leak their secrets. Nor do they like it when an agency takes credit for *their* success. To get between a client and the footlights is bad manners.

We have an infuriating habit of divine discontent with our performance. It is an antidote to smugness.

Our far-flung enterprise is held together by a network of personal friendships. We all belong to the same club.

We like reports and correspondence to be well written, easy to read – and *short*. We are revolted by pseudo-academic jargon, like "attitudinal," "paradigms," "demassification," "reconceptualize," "suboptimal," "symbiotic linkage," "splinterization," "dimensionalization." (Lord Rutherford used to tell his staff at the Cavendish Laboratory that if they couldn't explain their physics to a barmaid, it was bad physics.)

Through maddening repetition, some of my *obiter dicta* have been woven into our culture. Here are some of them:

(1) "We sell – or else."

(2) "You cannot *bore* people into buying your product; you can only *interest* them in buying it."

(3) "We prefer the discipline of knowledge to the anarchy of ignorance. We pursue knowledge the way a pig pursues truffles. A blind pig can sometimes find truffles, but it helps to know that they grow in oak forests."

(4) "We hire gentlemen with brains."

(5) "The consumer is not a moron. She is your wife. Don't insult her intelligence."

(6) "Unless your campaign contains a Big Idea, it will pass like a ship in the night." (I doubt if more than one campaign in a hundred contains a big idea. I am supposed to be one of the more fertile inventors of big ideas, but in my long career I have not had more than twenty.)

(7) "Only First Class business, and that in a First Class way."

(8) "Never run an advertisement you would not want your own family to see."

(9) "Search all the parks in all your cities; you'll find no statues of committees."

This book says nothing about "direct response" advertising, the kind which invites the reader to order the product by mail from the manufacturer. The people who write this kind of advertisement know exactly how many products they sell, whereas those who write "ordinary" advertisements and television commercials seldom, if ever, know; too many other factors are involved in the marketing mix, like price-off deals by competitors, and shrinkage in retailers' stocks.

The curious thing is that the techniques which work best in "direct" advertisements are seldom used in ordinary advertising – like giving factual information about the product.

If all advertisers were to follow the example of their direct response brethren, they would *sell* more. Every copywriter should start his or her career by spending two years in direct response.

One glance at any advertisement tells me whether the copywriter has ever had that experience.

Four Problems

Today, the world of advertising faces four problems of crisis dimensions.

The *first* problem is that manufacturers of package-goods products, which have always been the mainstay of advertising, are now spending twice as much on price-off deals as on advertising. They are buying volume by price discounting, instead of using advertising to build strong brands. Any damn fool can put on a price reduction, but it takes brains and perseverance to create a brand.

There used to be a popular brand of coffee called Chase & Sanborn. Then the manufacturers started price discounts. They became *addicted* to them. Where is that brand today? Dead as a doornail.

Listen to a speech I made in Chicago in 1955:

> "The time has come to *sound an alarm*, to warn manufacturers what is going to happen to their brands if they spend so much on deals that there is no money left for advertising to build their brand.

> "Deals don't build the kind of indestructible image which is the only thing that can make your brand part of the fabric of life."

Andrew Ehrenberg of the London Business School has one of the best brains in marketing today. He reports that a cut-price offer can induce people to try a brand, but they return to their habitual brands as if nothing had happened.

Why are so many brand managers addicted to price-cutting deals? Because the people who employ them are only interested in next quarter's profit. Why? Because they are more concerned with their stock options than the future of their company.

Price-off deals are a drug. Ask a drug-addicted brand manager what happened to his share of the market after the delirium of the deal subsided. He will change the subject. Ask him if the deal increased his *profit*. Again he will change the subject.

Marketers who have inherited brands built by their predecessors are dealing them to oblivion. Sooner or later they discover that they cannot deal brands which nobody has heard of. Brands are the seed corn they have inherited. They are eating their seed corn.

These cut-price boobies also have a habit of trying to cut the price of their agency's services. Clients who haggle over their agency's compensation are looking through the wrong end of the telescope. Instead of trying to shave a few measly cents off the agency's fifteen per cent, they should concentrate on getting more sales results from the eighty-five per cent they spend on time and space. That is where the leverage is. No manufacturer ever got rich by underpaying his agency. Pay peanuts and you get monkeys.

The *second* problem is that advertising agencies, notably in Britain, France, and the United States, are now infested with people who regard advertising as an avant-garde art form. They have never sold anything in their lives. Their ambition is to win awards at the Cannes Festival. They bamboozle their unfortunate clients into paying millions of dollars a year to exhibit their originality. They aren't interested in the products they advertise, and assume that the consumer won't be either; so they say almost nothing about their virtues. At best they are mere entertainers, and rather feeble ones at that. Many of them are art directors who, being visual-minded, don't read anything themselves and make it impossible for consumers to read the copy I write. At a luncheon recently I heard an angry manufacturer refer to these self-indulgent idiots as *mincing pansies*. Given my education, I might have fallen into this trap myself if I had not spent five years selling kitchen stoves door-to-door. Once a salesman, always a salesman.

The *third* problem is the emergence of megalomaniacs whose mind-set is more financial than creative. They are building empires by buying up other agencies, to the consternation of their clients.

The *fourth* problem is that advertising agencies still waste their clients' money repeating the same mistakes. I recently counted forty-nine advertisements set in reverse (white type on black background) in one issue of a German magazine, long years after research demonstrated that reverse is difficult to read.

During a ten-hour train ride, I read the ads in three magazines. Most of them violated elementary principles which were discovered in years gone by – and set out in *Confessions*. The copywriters and art directors who created them are ignorant amateurs.

What is the reason for their failure to study experience? Is it that advertising does not attract inquiring minds? Is it that any kind of scientific method is beyond their grasp? Are they afraid that knowledge would impose some discipline on them – or expose their incompetence?

My Last Will And Testament

I started my career in research with the great Dr. Gallup at Princeton. Then I became an advertising copywriter. As far as I know, I am the only "creative" hot-shot who started out in research. As a result, I look at the creative function through the objective eyes of a researcher. These are the most valuable lessons I have learned:

(1) Creating successful advertising is a craft, part inspiration but mostly know-how and hard work. If you have a modicum of talent, and know which techniques work at the cash register, you will go a long way.

(2) The temptation to entertain instead of selling is contagious.

(3) The difference between one advertisement and another, when measured in terms of sales, can be as much as nineteen to one.

(4) It pays to study the product before writing your advertisements.
(5) The key to success is to promise the *consumer a benefit* – like better flavor, whiter wash, more miles per gallon, a better complexion.

(6) The function of most advertising is not to persuade people to try your product, but to persuade them to use it more often than other brands in their repertoire. (Thank you, Andrew Ehrenberg.)

(7) What works in one country almost always works in other countries.

(8) Editors of magazines are better communicators than advertising people. Copy their techniques.

(9) Most campaigns are too complicated. They reflect a long list of objectives, and try to reconcile the divergent views of too many executives. By attempting to cover too many things, they achieve nothing. Their advertisements look like the minutes of a committee.

(10) Don't let men write advertising for products which are bought by women.

(11) Good campaigns can run for many years without losing their selling power. My eyepatch campaign for Hathaway shirts ran for twenty-one years. My campaign for Dove soap has been running for thirty-one years, and Dove is now the best seller.

Once a salesman, always a salesman.

David Ogilvy
1988

Confessions of an Advertising Man

Background

As a child I lived in Lewis Carroll's house in Guildford. My father, whom I adored, was a Gaelic-speaking highlander, a classical scholar, and a bigoted agnostic. One day he discovered that I had started going to church secretly.

"My dear old son, how can you swallow that mumbo-jumbo? It is all very well for servants, but not for educated people. *You don't have to be a Christian to behave like a gentleman!*"

My mother was a beautiful and eccentric Irishwoman. She disinherited me, on the ground that I was likely to acquire more money than was good for me, without any help from her. I could not disagree.

At the age of nine I was sent to board at an aristocratic Dotheboys Hall in Eastbourne. The headmaster wrote of me, "He has a distinctly original mind, inclined to argue with his teachers and to try and convince them that he is right and the books are wrong; but this perhaps is further proof of his originality." When I suggested that Napoleon might have been a Dutchman because his brother was King of Holland, the headmaster's wife sent me to bed without supper. When she was robing me for the part of the Abbess in *The Comedy of Errors*, I rehearsed my opening speech with an emphasis that she disliked; whereupon she seized me by the cheek and threw me to the floor.

At the age of thirteen I went to Fettes, a Scottish school whose Spartan disciplines had been established by my great-uncle Lord

Justice General Inglis, the greatest Scottish advocate of all time. My friends at this splendid school included Ian Macleod, Niall Macpherson, Knox Cunningham, and several other future Members of Parliament. Chief among the masters I remember Henry Havergal, who inspired me to play the double bass, and Walter Sellar, who wrote *1066 and All That* while teaching me history.

I made a botch of Oxford. Keith Feiling, the historian, had given me a scholarship at Christ Church, and I was the recipient of much kindness from Patrick Gordon-Walker, Roy Harrod, A. S. Russell, and other dons. But I was too preoccupied to do any work, and was duly expelled.

That was in 1931, the bottom of the depression. For the next seventeen years, while my friends were establishing themselves as doctors, lawyers, civil servants, and politicians, I adventured about the world, uncertain of purpose. I was a chef in Paris, a door-to-door salesman, a social worker in the Edinburgh slums, an associate of Dr. Gallup in research for the motion picture industry, an assistant to Sir William Stephenson in British Security Co-ordination, and a farmer in Pennsylvania.

My boyhood hero had been Lloyd George, and I had expected to become Prime Minister when I grew up. Instead, I finally became an advertising agent on Madison Avenue; the revenues of my nineteen clients are now greater than the revenue of Her Majesty's Government.

Max Beerbohm once told S. N. Behrman, "If I was endowed with wealth I should start a great advertising campaign in all the principal newspapers. The advertisements would consist of one short sentence, printed in huge block letters – a sentence that I once heard spoken by a husband to a wife: *'My dear, nothing in this world is worth buying.'"*

My position is the opposite. I want to buy almost everything I see advertised. My father used to say of a product that it was "very well spoken of in the advertisements." I spend my life speaking well of products in advertisements; I hope that you get as much pleasure out of buying them as I get out of advertising them.

By writing this book in the old-fashioned first person singular, I have committed an offense against a convention of contemporary American manners. But I think it artificial to write *we* when I am confessing *my* sins and describing *my* adventures.

David Ogilvy
Ipswich, Massachusetts

1 How to Manage an Advertising Agency

Managing an advertising agency is like managing any other creative organization – a research laboratory, a magazine, an architect's office, a great kitchen.

Thirty years ago I was a chef at the Hotel Majestic in Paris. Henri Soulé of the Pavillon tells me that it was probably the best kitchen there has ever been.

There were thirty-seven chefs in our brigade. We worked like dervishes, sixty-three hours a week – there was no trade union. From morning to night we sweated and shouted and cursed and cooked. Every man jack was inspired by one ambition: to cook better than any chef had ever cooked before. Our *esprit de corps* would have done credit to the Marines.

I have always believed that if I could understand how Monsieur Pitard, the head chef, inspired such white-hot morale, I could apply the same kind of leadership to the management of my advertising agency.

To begin with, he was the best cook in the whole brigade, and we knew it. He had to spend most of his time at his desk, planning menus, scrutinizing bills, and ordering supplies, but once a week he would emerge from his glass-walled office in the middle of the kitchen and actually *cook* something. A crowd of us always gathered around to watch, spellbound by his virtuosity. It was inspiring to work for a supreme master.

(Following Chef Pitard's example, I still write occasional advertisements myself, to remind my brigade of copywriters that my hand has not lost its cunning.)

M. Pitard ruled with a rod of iron, and we were terrified of him. There he sat in his glass cage, the *gros bonnet*, the arch symbol of authority. Whenever I made a mistake in my work, I would look up to see if his gimlet eye had noticed it.

Cooks, like copywriters, work under ferocious pressures, and are apt to be quarrelsome. I doubt whether a more easygoing boss could have prevented our rivalries from breaking into violence. M. Bourgignon, our *chef saucier*, told me that by the time a cook is forty, he is either dead or crazy. I understood what he meant the night our *chef potagier* threw forty-seven raw eggs across the kitchen at my head, scoring nine direct hits; his patience had been exhausted by my raids on his stock pot in search of bones for the poodles of an important client.

Our *chef pâtissier* was equally eccentric. Every night he left the kitchen with a chicken concealed in the crown of his Homburg hat. When he went on vacation he made me stuff two dozen peaches into the legs of his long underwear. But when the King and Queen of England were given a state dinner at Versailles, this roguish genius was chosen from all the *pâtissiers* in France to prepare the ornamental baskets of sugar and the *petits fours glacés*.

M. Pitard praised very seldom, but when he did, we were exalted to the skies. When the President of France came to a banquet at the Majestic, the atmosphere in our kitchen was electric. On one of these memorable occasions, I was covering frogs' legs with a white chaud-froid sauce, decorating each little thigh with an ornate leaf of chervil. Suddenly I became aware that M. Pitard was standing beside me, watching. I was so frightened that my knees knocked together and my hands trembled. He took the pencil from his starched toque and waved it in the air, his signal for the whole brigade to gather. Then he pointed at my frogs' legs and said, very slowly and very quietly, "That's how to do it." I was his slave for life.

(Today I praise my staff as rarely as Pitard praised his chefs, in the hope that they too will appreciate it more than a steady gush of appreciation.)

M. Pitard gave us all a great sense of occasion. One evening when I had prepared a Soufflé Rothschild (with three liqueurs) he took me upstairs to the door of the dining room and allowed me to watch President Paul Doumer eat it. Three weeks later, on May 7, 1932, Doumer was dead.*

(I find that people who work in my agency get a similar charge out of state occasions. When a crisis keeps them working all night, their morale is high for weeks afterward.)

M. Pitard did not tolerate incompetence. He knew that it is demoralizing for professionals to work alongside incompetent amateurs. I saw him fire three pastry-cooks in a month for the same crime: they could not make the caps on their brioches rise evenly. Mr. Gladstone would have applauded such ruthlessness; he held that the "first essential for a Prime Minister is to be a good butcher."

M. Pitard taught me exorbitant standards of service. For example,

* Not from my soufflé, but from the bullet of a mad Russian.

he once heard me tell a waiter that we were fresh out of the *plat du jour* – and almost fired me for it. In a great kitchen, he said, one must always honor what one has promised on the menu. I pointed out that the dish in question would take so long to cook that no client would wait for a new batch to be prepared. Was it our famous *coulibiac de saumon*, a complicated kedgeree made with the spine marrow of sturgeon, semolina kache, salmon collops, mushrooms, onions, and rice, rolled up in a brioche paste and baked for fifty minutes? Or was it our still more exotic Karoly Éclairs, stuffed with a purée of woodcocks' entrails cooked in champagne, covered with a brown *chaud-froid* sauce and masked with game jelly? At this distance of time, I do not remember, but I remember exactly what Pitard said to me: "Next time you see that we are running out of a *plat du jour*, come and tell me. I will then get on the telephone to other hotels and restaurants until I find one which has the same dish on its menu. Then I will send you in a taxi to bring back a supply. Never again tell a waiter that we are fresh out of anything."

(Today I see red when anybody at Ogilvy, Benson & Mather tells a client that we cannot produce an advertisement or a television commercial on the day we have promised it. In the best establishments, promises are always kept, whatever it may cost in agony and overtime.)

Soon after I joined M. Pitard's brigade I was faced with a problem in morality for which neither my father nor my schoolmasters had prepared me. The *chef garde-manger* sent me to the *chef saucier* with some raw sweetbreads which smelled so putrid that I knew they would endanger the life of any client who ate them; the sauce would mask their condition, and the client would eat them. I protested to the *chef garde-manger*, but he told me to carry out his order; he knew that he would be in hot water if M. Pitard discovered that he had run out of fresh sweetbreads. What was I to do? I had been brought up to believe that it is dishonorable to inform. But I did just that. I took the putrid sweetbreads to M. Pitard, and invited him to smell them. Without a word to me, he went over to the *chef garde-manger* and fired him. The poor bastard had to leave, then and there.

In *Down and Out in Paris and London* George Orwell told the world that French kitchens are dirty. He had never worked at the Majestic. M. Pitard was a martinet in making us keep the kitchen clean. Twice a day I had to scrape the wooden surface of the larder table with a sharp plane. Twice a day the floor was scrubbed, and clean sawdust put down. Once a week a bugcatcher scoured the kitchen in search of roaches. We were issued clean uniforms every morning.

(Today I am a martinet in making my staff keep their offices shipshape. A messy office creates an atmosphere of sloppiness, and leads to the disappearance of secret papers.)

We cooks were badly paid, but M. Pitard made so much from the commissions which his suppliers paid him that he could afford to live in a château. Far from concealing his wealth from the rest of us, he drove to work in a taxi, carried a cane with a gold head, and dressed, when off-duty, like an international banker. This flaunting of privilege stimulated our ambition to follow in his footsteps.

The immortal Auguste Escoffier had the same idea. When he was *Chef des Cuisines* at the Carlton in London before the First World War, he used to drive to the Derby on the box of a coach-and-four, dressed in a gray frock coat and top hat. Among my fellow cooks at the Majestic, Escoffier's *Guide Culinaire* was still the definitive authority, the court of last appeal in all our arguments about recipes. Just before he died he emerged from retirement and came to luncheon in our kitchen; it was like Brahms lunching with the musicians of the Philharmonic.

During the service of luncheon and dinner, M. Pitard stationed himself at the counter where we cooks handed our dishes to the waiters. He inspected every single dish before it left the kitchen. Sometimes he sent it back to the cook for more work. Always he reminded us not to put too much on the plate – "*pas trop!*" He wanted the Majestic to make a profit.

(Today I inspect every campaign before it goes to the client, and send back many of them for more work. And I share M. Pitard's passion for profit.)

Perhaps the ingredient in M. Pitard's leadership which made the most profound impression on me was his industry. I found my sixty-three hours bending over a red-hot stove so exhausting that I had to spend my day off lying on my back in a meadow, looking at the sky. But Pitard worked *seventy-seven* hours a week, and took only one free day a fortnight.

(That is about my schedule today. I figure that my staff will be less reluctant to work overtime if I work longer hours than they do. An executive who recently left my agency wrote in his farewell letter, "You set the pace on doing homework. It is a disconcerting experience to spend a Saturday evening in the garden next door to your house, carousing for four hours while you sit, unmoving, at your desk by the window doing your homework. The word gets around.")

I learned something else at the Majestic: If you can make yourself indispensable to a client, you will never be fired. Our most important client, an American lady who occupied a suite of seven rooms, subjected herself to a diet which was based on a baked apple at every meal. One day she threatened to move to the Ritz unless her apple was always *burst*. I developed a technique of baking *two* apples, passing their flesh through a sieve to remove all traces of core, and then replacing the flesh of both apples in one skin. The result was the most voluptuous baked apple our client had ever seen, and more calories than she ever suspected. Word came down to the kitchen that the chef who was baking those apples must be given tenure.

My closest friend was an elderly *argentier* who bore a striking resemblance to the late Charles C. Burlingham. His most cherished memory was a vision of Edward VII (Edward the Caressor) floating majestically across the sidewalk to his brougham after two magnums of *entente cordiale* at Maxim's. My friend was a Communist. Nobody cared about that; they were far more impressed by my own nationality. A Scotsman in a French kitchen is as rare as a Scotsman on Madison Avenue. My fellow chefs, who had heard tales of my ancestral Highlands, christened me *Sauvage*.

I became still more *sauvage* when I arrived on Madison Avenue. Managing an advertising agency isn't all beer and skittles. After fourteen years of it, I have come to the conclusion that the top man has one principal responsibility: to provide an atmosphere in which creative mavericks can do useful work. Dr. William Menninger has described the difficulties with uncanny insight:

> In the advertising industry to be successful you must, of necessity, accumulate a group of creative people. This probably means a fairly high percentage of high strung, brilliant, eccentric nonconformists.

Like most doctors, you are on call day and night, seven days a week. This constant pressure on every advertising executive must take a considerable physical and psychological toll – the pressure that the executive places on the account executive, on the supervisor, and they in turn on the creative people. Then, most of all, the clients' pressures on them and on you.

A special problem with the employees of an advertising agency is that each one watches the other one very carefully to see if one gets a carpet before the other, to see if one has an assistant before the other, or to see if one makes an extra nickel before the other. It isn't that they want the carpet or the assistant or the nickel so much as it is the recognition of their "standing with father."

The executive is inevitably a father figure. To be a good father, whether it is to his children or to his associates, requires that he be understanding, that he be considerate, and that he be human enough to be *affectionate*.

In the early days of our agency I worked cheek by jowl with every employee; communication and affection were easy. But as our brigade grows bigger I find it more difficult. How can I be a father figure to people who don't even know me by sight? My agency now employs 497 men and women. I have discovered that they have an average of one hundred friends each – a total of 49,700 friends. If I tell all my staff what we are doing in the agency, what we believe in, what our ambitions are, they will tell their 49,700 friends. And this will give us 49,700 rooters for Ogilvy, Benson & Mather.

So once a year I assemble the whole brigade in the auditorium of the Museum of Modern Art, and give them a candid report on our operations, profits and all. Then I tell them what kind of behavior I admire, in these terms:

(1) I admire people who work hard, who bite the bullet. I dislike passengers who don't pull their weight in the boat. It is more fun to be overworked than to be underworked. There is an economic factor built into hard work. The harder you work, the fewer employees we need, and the more profit we make. The more profit we make, the more money becomes available for all of us.

(2) I admire people with first-class brains, because you cannot run a great advertising agency without brainy people. But brains are not enough unless they are combined with *intellectual honesty*.

(3) I have an inviolable rule against employing nepots and spouses, because they breed politics. Whenever two of our people get married, one of them must depart – preferably the female, to look after her baby.

(4) I admire people who work with gusto. If you don't enjoy what you are doing, I beg you to find another job. Remember the Scottish proverb, "Be happy while you're living, for you're a long time dead."

(5) I despise toadies who suck up to their bosses; they are generally the same people who bully their subordinates.

(6) I admire self-confident professionals, the craftsmen who do their jobs with superlative excellence. They always seem to respect the expertise of their colleagues. They don't poach.

(7) I admire people who hire subordinates who are good enough

to succeed them. I pity people who are so insecure that they feel compelled to hire inferiors as their subordinates.

(8) I admire people who build up their subordinates, because this is the only way we can promote from within the ranks. I detest having to go outside to fill important jobs, and I look forward to the day when that will never be necessary.

(9) I admire people with gentle manners who treat other people as human beings. I abhor quarrelsome people. I abhor people who wage paper-warfare. The best way to keep the peace is to be candid. Remember Blake:

> I was angry with my friend;
> I told my wrath, my wrath did end.
> I was angry with my foe;
> I told it not, my wrath did grow.

(10) I admire well-organized people who deliver their work on time. The Duke of Wellington never went home until he had finished *all* the work on his desk.

Having told my staff what I expect of them, I then tell them what I expect of myself:

(1) I try to be fair and to be firm, to make unpopular decisions without cowardice, to create an atmosphere of stability, and to listen more than I talk.

(2) I try to sustain the momentum of the agency – its ferment, its vitality, its forward thrust.

(3) I try to build the agency by landing new accounts. (At this

point the upturned faces in my audience look like baby birds
waiting for the father bird to feed them.)

(4) I try to win the confidence of our clients at their highest level.

(5) I try to make sufficient profits to keep you all from penury in
old age.

(6) I plan our policies far into the future.

(7) I try to recruit people of the highest quality at all levels, to
build the hottest staff in the agency business.

(8) I try to get the best out of every man and woman in the agency.

Running an agency takes vitality, and sufficient resilience to pick
oneself up after defeats. Affection for one's henchmen, and toler-
ance for their foibles. A genius for composing sibling rivalries. An
unerring eye for the main chance. And morality – people who
work in advertising agencies can suffer serious blows to their *esprit
de corps* if they catch their leader in acts of unprincipled oppor-
tunism.

Above all, the head of an agency must know how to delegate.
This is easier said than done. The clients don't like the management of their accounts to be delegated to juniors, any more than
patients in hospitals like the doctors to turn them over to
medical students.

In my opinion, delegation has been carried too far in some of the
big agencies. Their top men have withdrawn into administration,
leaving all contact with clients to juniors. This process builds large

agencies, but it leads to mediocrity in performance. I have no ambition to preside over a vast bureaucracy. That is why we have only nineteen clients. The pursuit of excellence is less profitable than the pursuit of bigness, but it can be more satisfying.

The act of delegation often results in interposing a foreman between the agency boss and his staff. When this happens, the employees feel like children whose mother turns them over to the tender mercies of a nanny. But they become reconciled to the separation when they discover that the nannies are more patient, more accessible, and more expert than I am.

My success or failure as the head of an agency depends more than anything else on my ability to find people who can create great campaigns, men with fire in their bellies. Creativity has become the subject of formal study by psychologists. If they can identify the characteristics of creative individuals, they can put into my hands a psychometric test for selecting young people who can be taught to become great campaign-builders. Dr. Frank Barron at the University of California's Institute of Personality Assessment has done promising research in this direction. His conclusions fit my own observations:

> Creative people are especially observant, and they value accurate observation (telling themselves the truth) more than other people do.

> They often express part-truths, but this they do vividly; the part they express is the generally unrecognized; by displacement of accent and apparent disproportion in statement they seek to point to the usually unobserved. They see things as others do, but also as others do not.

They are born with greater brain capacity; they have more ability to hold many ideas at once, and to compare more ideas with one another – hence to make a richer synthesis.

They are by constitution more vigorous, and have available to them an exceptional fund of psychic and physical energy.

Their universe is thus more complex, and in addition they usually lead more complex lives.

They have more contact than most people do with the life of the unconscious – with fantasy, reverie, the world of imagination.*

While I wait for Dr. Barron and his colleagues to synthesize their clinical observations into formal psychometric tests, I have to rely on more old-fashioned and empirical techniques for spotting creative dynamos. Whenever I see a remarkable advertisement or television commercial, I find out who wrote it. Then I call the writer on the telephone and congratulate him on his work. A poll has shown that creative people would rather work at Ogilvy, Benson & Mather than at any other agency, so my telephone call often produces an application for a job.

I then ask the candidate to send me the six best advertisements and commercials he has ever written. This reveals, among other things, whether he can recognize a good advertisement when he sees one, or is only the instrument of an able supervisor. Sometimes I call on my victim at home; ten minutes after crossing the threshold I can

---

* "The Psychology of Imagination" by Frank Barron, *Scientific American* (September 1958).

tell whether he has a richly furnished mind, what kind of taste he has, and whether he is happy enough to sustain pressure.

We receive hundreds of job applications every year. I am particularly interested in those which come from the Middle West. I would rather hire an ambitious young man from Des Moines than a high-priced fugitive from a fashionable agency on Madison Avenue. When I observe these grandees, coldly correct and critically dull, I am reminded of Roy Campbell's "On Some South African Novelists":

> You praise the firm restraint with which they write
> I'm with you there, of course.
> They use the snaffle and the curb all right;
> But where's the bloody horse?

I pay special attention to applications from Western Europe. Some of our best writers are Europeans. They are well educated, they work hard, they are less conventional, and they are more objective in their approach to the American consumer.

Advertising is a business of *words*, but advertising agencies are infested with men and women who cannot write. They cannot write advertisements, and they cannot write plans. They are as helpless as deaf mutes on the stage of the Metropolitan Opera.

It is sad that the majority of men who are responsible for advertising today, both the agents and the clients, are so conventional. The business community wants remarkable advertising, but turns a cold shoulder to the kind of people who can produce it. That is why most advertisements are so infernally dull. Albert Lasker made $50,000,000 out of advertising, partly because he could stomach the atrocious manners of his great copywriters – John E. Kennedy, Claude C. Hopkins, and Frank Hummert.

Some of the mammoth agencies are now being managed by second-generation caretakers who floated to the top of their organizations because they were smooth contact men. But courtiers cannot create potent campaigns. The sad truth is that despite the sophisticated apparatus of the modern agency, advertising isn't getting the results it used to get in the crude days of Lasker and Hopkins. Our business needs massive transfusions of *talent* . . . And talent, I believe, is most likely to be found among nonconformists, dissenters, and rebels.

Not long ago the University of Chicago invited me to participate in a seminar on the Creative Organization. Most of the other participants were learned professors of psychology who make it their business to study what they call CREATIVITY. Feeling like a pregnant woman at a convention of obstetricians, I told them what I have learned about the creative process from my experience as the chief of seventy-three writers and artists.

The creative process requires more than reason. Most original thinking isn't even verbal. It requires "a groping experimentation with ideas, governed by intuitive hunches and inspired by the unconscious." The majority of business men are incapable of original thinking because they are unable to escape from the tyranny of reason. Their imaginations are blocked.

I am almost incapable of logical thought, but I have developed techniques for keeping open the telephone line to my unconscious, in case that disorderly repository has anything to tell me. I hear a great deal of music. I am on friendly terms with John Barleycorn. I take long hot baths. I garden. I go into retreat among the Amish. I watch birds. I go for long walks in the country. And I take frequent vacations, so that my brain can lie fallow – no golf, no cocktail parties, no tennis, no bridge, no concentration; only a bicycle.

While thus employed in doing nothing, I receive a constant stream of telegrams from my unconscious, and these become the raw material for my advertisements. But more is required: hard work, an open mind, and ungovernable curiosity.

Many of the greatest creations of man have been inspired by the desire to make *money*. When George Frederick Handel was on his beam ends, he shut himself up for twenty-one days and emerged with the complete score of *Messiah* – and hit the jackpot. Few of the themes of *Messiah* were original; Handel dredged them up from his unconscious, where they had been stored since he heard them in other composers' work, or since he had composed them for his own forgotten operas.

At the end of a concert at Carnegie Hall, Walter Damrosch asked Rachmaninoff what sublime thoughts had passed through his head as he stared out into the audience during the playing of his concerto. "I was counting the house," said Rachmaninoff.

If Oxford undergraduates were *paid* for their work, I would have performed miracles of scholarship and become Regius Professor of Modern History; it wasn't until I tasted lucre on Madison Avenue that I began to work in earnest.

In the modern world of business, it is useless to be a creative, original thinker unless you can also *sell* what you create. Management cannot be expected to recognize a good idea unless it is presented

to them by a good salesman. In my fourteen years on Madison
Avenue I have had only one great idea which I was unable to sell.
(I wanted International Paper to dedicate their 26,000,000 acres of
woodlands to the public for camping, fishing, hunting, hiking, and
bird-watching. I suggested that this sublime gesture would rank
with Carnegie's libraries and Rockefeller's foundation as an act of
historic munificence. It is a good idea, but I failed to sell it.)

Finally, I have observed that no creative organization, whether it is
a research laboratory, a magazine, a Paris kitchen, or an advertising agency, will produce a great body of work *unless it is led by a
formidable individual.*. The Cavendish Laboratory at Cambridge was
great because of Lord Rutherford. The *New Yorker* was great
because of Ross. The Majestic was great because of Pitard.

It isn't everybody who enjoys working in the *atelier* of a master. The
implication of dependence gnaws at their vitals, until they conclude:

> To reign is worth ambition though in Hell:
> Better to reign in Hell, than serve in Heaven.

So they leave my *atelier*, only to discover that their paradise is lost.
A few weeks after one of these poor fellows departed, he wrote:
"When I left your agency I was prepared to feel some sadness.
What I felt was distress. I have never been so bereft in all my life.
This I suppose is the price one has to pay for the privilege of
having belonged to an élite. There are so few of them around."

When a good man quits, his cronies wonder why, and generally
suspect that he has been mistreated by management. Recently I
have found a way to prevent this misunderstanding. When my
young copy chief resigned to become Vice Chairman of another

agency, he and I exchanged letters in the style of a cabinet minister resigning to a Prime Minister, and they were printed in our staff magazine. The dear defector wrote to me:

> You must accept the blame for what I am as an advertising man. You invented me and have taught me how much I do not know. You once said that you should have charged me tuition all these years, and it's true.

I replied in kind:

> It has been a grand experience to watch you grow in eleven short years from cub writer to Copy Chief. You have become one of our best campaign-builders.

> You work hard, and you work fast. Your vitality and resilience make it possible for you to remain calm and cheerful – *contagiously* cheerful – through all the tribulations which buffet copy chiefs.

Few of the great creators have bland personalities. They are cantankerous egotists, the kind of men who are unwelcome in the modern corporation. Consider Winston Churchill. He drank like a fish. He was capricious and willful. When opposed, he sulked. He was rude to fools. He was wildly extravagant. He wept on the slightest provocation. His conversation was Rabelaisian. He was inconsiderate to his staff. Yet Lord Alanbrooke, his Chief of Staff, could write:

I shall always look back on the years I worked with him as some of the most difficult and trying ones in my life. For all that I thank God that I was given the opportunity of working alongside of such a man, and of having my eyes opened to the fact that occasionally such supermen exist on this earth.

II How to Get Clients

Fifteen years ago I was an obscure tobacco farmer in Pennsylvania. Today I preside over one of the best advertising agencies in the United States, with billings of $55,000,000 a year, a payroll of $5,000,000, and offices in New York, Chicago, Los Angeles, San Francisco, and Toronto.

How did this come to pass? As my Amish friends have said, "It wonders me."

On the day in 1948 when I hung out my shingle, I issued the following Order of the Day:

> This is a new agency, struggling for its life. For some time we shall be overworked and underpaid.

> In hiring, the emphasis will be on *youth* . . . We are looking for young turks. I have no use for toadies or hacks. I seek gentlemen with brains.

> Agencies are as big as they deserve to be. We are starting this one on a shoestring, but we are going to make it a great agency before 1960.

The next day I made a list of the five clients I wanted most: General Foods, Bristol-Myers, Campbell Soup Company, Lever Brothers, and Shell.*

---

* To pick such blue-chip targets was an act of mad presumption, but all five of them are now clients of Ogilvy, Benson & Mather.

In the old days it had not been unknown for advertisers of this magnitude to engage dark-horse agencies. When the head of a mammoth agency solicited the Camel Cigarette account, he promised to assign *thirty* copywriters to it, but the canny head of R. J. Reynolds replied, *"How about one good one?"* Then he gave his account to a young copywriter called Bill Esty, in whose agency it has remained for twenty-eight years.

In 1937 Walter Chrysler gave the Plymouth account to Sterling Getchel, then in his thirty-second year. In 1940 Ed Little gave most of the Colgate account to a dark-horse named Ted Bates. And General Foods discovered Young & Rubicam when that agency was only one year old. Writing after his retirement, John Orr Young, one of the founders of Young & Rubicam, offered this advice to manufacturers in search of an agency:

If you are lucky enough to find some young men with that special energy and daring which leads them into business for themselves, you will benefit from having that incalculably valuable quality serving you.

It is easy to be beguiled by acres of desks, departments, and other big agency appurtenances. What counts is the real *motive* power of the agency, the *creative potency.*

Several great advertising successes have been achieved by advertisers who benefited by the incentive, ambition and energy of an advertising organization in process of building a reputation.

These large advertisers sought to buy their advertising agency service on a rising market, during the agent's workclothes days or pre-adipose period.*

By the time I came on the scene, the big advertisers had grown more cautious. God had joined the side of the big battalions. Stanley Resor, who had been head of J. Walter Thompson since 1916, warned me, "The concentration of industry into huge corporations is being reflected in the world of advertising. The big accounts now require such a wide range of services that only the huge agencies can handle them. Why don't you give up your pipe dream and join J. Walter Thompson?"

To new agencies about to embark on the pursuit of their first clients, I bequeath a set-piece which worked magic in my early days. I used to ask prospective clients to ponder the life cycle of a typical agency, the inevitable pattern of rise and decline, from dynamite to dry rot:

Once every few years a great new agency is born. It is ambitious, hard working, full of dynamite. It gets accounts from soft old agencies. It does great work.

The years pass. The founders get rich, and tired. Their creative fires go out. They become extinct volcanoes.

The agency may continue to prosper. Its original momentum is not yet spent. It has powerful contacts. But it has grown too big. It produces dull, routine campaigns, based on the echo of old victories. Dry rot sets in. The emphasis shifts to collateral services, to conceal the agency's creative bankruptcy. At

---

* John Orr Young, *Adventures in Advertising*, Harper, 1948.

this stage, it begins losing accounts to vital new agencies, ruthless upstarts who work hard and put all their dynamite into their advertisements.

We can all name famous agencies which are moribund. You hear demoralizing whispers in their corridors, long before the truth dawns on their clients.

At this point I could always see my prospective client struggling to conceal the fact that I had hit a nerve. Could it be that I was describing *his* moribund agency?

Today, fourteen years later, I am shocked by this villainous stratagem. My scholarly uncle Sir Humphry Rolleston used to say of physicians, "First they get *on*, then they get *honor*, then they get *honest*." I am now approaching the stage of honesty, and butter wouldn't melt in my mouth. But everything looked different when my bank account was empty. As Gilbert's Pirate King explained:

> When I sally forth to seek my prey
> I help myself in a royal way:
> I sink a few more ships, it's true,
> Than a well-bred monarch ought to do;
> But many a king on a first-class throne,
> If he wants to call his crown his own,
> Must manage somehow to get through
> More dirty work than ever *I* do.

Following Henry Ford's advice to his dealers that they should "solicit by personal visitation," I started by soliciting advertisers who did not employ an agency at all, figuring that I lacked the credentials to push any incumbent agency out of bed. My first target was Wedgwood China, which spent about $40,000 a year. Mr. Wedgwood and his advertising manageress received me with the greatest civility.

"We dislike agencies," she said. "They are nothing but a nuisance. So we prepare our own advertisements. Do you have any fault to find with them?"

"On the contrary," I replied, "I admire them. But if you will just allow me to buy the space for you, the magazines will give me the commission. It will cost you nothing, and I will promise never to darken your door again."

Hensleigh Wedgwood is a kindly man, and the next morning he wrote me a formal letter of appointment, to which I replied by telegram, "A Full Peel of Kent Treble Bob Major."* We were in business.

But my capital was only $6,000 and this was scarcely enough to keep me afloat until the first commissions arrived. Fortunately for me, my elder brother Francis was then Managing Director of Mather & Crowther Ltd., a venerable and distinguished advertising agency in London. He came to the rescue by persuading his partners to augment my capital and lend me their name. My old friend Bobby Bevan of S. H. Benson Ltd., another English agency, followed suit, and Sir Francis Meynell got Sir Stafford Cripps to authorize the transatlantic investment.

Bobby and Francis insisted that I find an American to be head of the

---

* It took Dorothy Sayers' Lord Peter Wimsey and his fellow change-ringers all night to ring this intricate peal of bells in the parish church of Fenchurch St. Paul.

agency. They did not believe that one of their fellow countrymen could persuade American manufacturers to give him any business. To expect an Englishman, or even a Scotsman, to be successful in American advertising would be absurd; advertising was not part of the British genius. Indeed, the British had always abhorred the whole idea of advertising. As *Punch* put it in 1848: "Let us be a nation of shopkeepers as much as we please, but there is no necessity that we should become a nation of advertisers." Out of 5,500 knights, baronets, and peers alive today, only *one* is an advertising agent.

(Prejudice against advertising and its practitioners is less marked in the United States. Neil McElroy, a former advertising manager of Procter & Gamble, was appointed Secretary of Defense in Eisenhower's administration. Chester Bowles graduated from Madison Avenue to become Governor of Connecticut, Ambassador to India, and Under Secretary of State. But even in the United States it is rare for advertising men to be appointed to important jobs in government. This is a pity, because some of them carry more guns than most of the lawyers, professors, bankers, and journalists who are favored. Senior advertising men are better equipped to define problems and opportunities; to set up short-range and long-range goals; to measure results; to lead large executive forces; to make lucid presentations to committees; and to operate within the disciplines of a budget. Observation of my elders and betters in other advertising agencies leads me to believe that many of them are more objective, better organized, more vigorous, and harder-working than their opposite numbers in legal practice, teaching, banking, and journalism.)

I had very little to offer the kind of American executive who would qualify to head up an agency. However, after casting about for several months, I invited Anderson Hewitt to leave the Chicago office of J. Walter Thompson and become my boss.

He was a dynamo of energy, he was unabashed in the presence of nabobs, and he had connections whose influence made my mouth water.

Within one year Andy Hewitt brought in two splendid accounts. With the help of John La Farge, who was billed as our copy chief, he landed Sunoco. And three months later his father-in-law Arthur Page induced the Chase Bank to hire us. When we ran out of capital, Andy Hewitt persuaded J. P. Morgan & Company to lend us $100,000 with no security except the confidence of his uncle Leffingwell, who was then Chairman of Morgan.

Alas, my partnership with Andy was not a happy one. We tried to conceal our differences from the staff, but children always know when their parents are at loggerheads. After four years of discord, exacerbated by the pressures of our meteoric success, the agency began to split into two factions. After much agony for all concerned, Andy resigned and I became head of the agency. I take comfort from the fact that he went on to great things at other agencies, unencumbered by an insufferable partner.

When we started our agency, we placed ourselves in competition with 3,000 other agencies. Our first job was to escape from obscurity, so that prospective clients would add us to their shopping lists. We succeeded in doing this faster than I had dared hope, and it may be helpful to other adventurers if I describe how we went about it.

First, I invited ten reporters from the advertising trade press to luncheon. I told them of my insane ambition to build a major agency from scratch. From that point on they gave me priceless tips on new business, and printed every release I sent them, however trivial; bless them. Rosser Reeves protested that nobody went to the bathroom at our agency without the news appearing in the trade press.

Second, I followed Edward L. Bernays' advice to make no more than two speeches a year. Every speech I made was calculated to provoke the greatest possible stir on Madison Avenue. The first was a lecture to the Art Directors Club in which I unloaded everything I knew about the graphics of advertising. Before going home, I gave each art director in my audience a mimeographed list of thirty-nine rules for making good layouts. Those ancient rules are still being passed around on Madison Avenue.

In my next speech I denounced the fatuity of the advertising courses being offered in colleges, and offered $10,000 to help start a college of advertising which would issue licenses to practice. This idiotic proposal hit the front pages. Soon the trade press took to calling me for comment on most of the issues that came up. I always spoke my mind, and I was always quoted.

Third, I made friends with men whose jobs brought them into contact with major advertisers – the researchers, the public relations consultants, the management engineers, and the space salesmen. They saw in me a possible source of future business for themselves, but what they got was a pitch on the merits of our agency.

Fourth, I sent frequent progress reports to 600 people in every walk of life. This barrage of direct mail was read by the most august advertisers. For example, when I solicited part of the Seagram account, Sam Bronfman played back to me the last two paragraphs of a sixteen-page speech I had sent him shortly before; and he hired us.

Gentle reader, if you are shocked by these confessions of self-advertisement, I can only plead that if I had behaved in a more professional way, it would have taken me twenty years to arrive. I had neither the time nor the money to wait. I was poor, unknown, and in a hurry.

Meanwhile, I was working from dawn until midnight, six days a week, creating campaigns for the clients who hired our infant agency. Some of those campaigns made advertising history.

At first we took every account we could get – a toy tortoise, a patent hairbrush, an English motorcycle. But I always kept my eye on my list of five blue-chip targets, and put our meager profits to work building the kind of organization which, I thought, would ultimately attract their attention.

I always showed prospective clients the dramatic improvement that followed when Ogilvy, Benson & Mather took accounts away from old agencies – "in every case we have blazed new trails, and in every case *sales have gone up.*" But I was never able to keep a straight face when I said this; if a company's sales had not grown more than sixfold in the previous twenty-one years, its growth had been less than average.

Some very ordinary agencies had the good fortune to hold portfolios of very ordinary accounts in 1945. All they had to do was fasten their seat belts and be lofted to enormous heights on the curve of a skyrocketing economy. It takes extraordinary ability for an agency to get accounts when everybody's sales are booming, but when the economy is jolted by a recession, the old fossils come unstuck, and vigorous new agencies leap forward.

An agency's first clients are the hardest to get, because it has no credentials, no record of success, no reputation. At this stage it often pays to speculate by conducting a pilot survey on some aspect of your prospective client's business. There are few manufacturers whose curiosity is not piqued when you offer to show them the results of such a survey.

The first time I tried this was with Helena Rubinstein, who had changed agencies seventeen times in the previous twenty-five years. Her account was then being handled by an agency which belonged to her younger son, Horace Titus. Our speculative research revealed that his advertising was ineffectual.

Madame Rubinstein showed no interest in the results of our research, but when I uncorked some advertisements based on it, she perked up, showing particular interest in photographs of my wife taken before and after treatment in the Rubinstein Salon. "I think your wife looked better *before*," said Madame.

To my amazement, Horace Titus advised his mother to remove her account from the agency he owned, and give it to me. This she did. Horace and I became friends, and remained so until his death eight years later.

In 1958 we were invited by Standard Oil (New Jersey) to show them what kind of advertising we would run if they were to hire us. Ten days later I presented them with a hamper of fourteen different campaigns, and won the account. Next to luck, fertility and midnight oil are the best weapons to use in hunting new business.

We spent $30,000 on a speculative presentation to Bromo Seltzer. It was based on a cogently argued thesis that the majority of headaches are of psychosomatic origin. But LeMoyne Billings, who was then Bromo Seltzer's advertising manager, preferred a presentation made by Lennen & Newell.

Today we have neither the time nor the stomach to prepare speculative campaigns. Instead, we show our prospects what we have done for other manufacturers, we explain our policies, and we introduce our department heads. We try to reveal ourselves as we really are, warts and all. If the prospective client likes the look of us, he hires us. If he doesn't like the look of us, we are better off without him.

When KLM Royal Dutch Airlines decided to change agencies, they invited Ogilvy, Benson & Mather and four others to prepare speculative campaigns. We were first on their tour of inspection. I opened the meeting by saying, "We have prepared nothing. Instead we would like you to tell us about your problems. Then you can visit the other four agencies on your list. They have all prepared speculative campaigns. If you like any of them, your choice will be easy. If you don't, come back and hire us. We will then embark on the research which always precedes the preparation of advertisements at our agency."

The Dutchmen accepted this bleak proposition, and five days later, after seeing the speculative campaigns prepared by the other agencies, they came back and hired us. To my great joy.

You cannot generalize. In some cases it pays to show speculative advertisements, as with Jersey and Helena Rubinstein. In some cases, it pays to be the one agency which refuses to do so, as with KLM. The agencies which are most successful in new business are those whose spokesmen show the most sensitive insight into the psychological make-up of the prospective client. Rigidity and sales-manship do not combine.

There is one stratagem which seems to work in almost every case: get the prospect to do most of the talking. The more you listen, the wiser he thinks you are. One day I went to see Alexander Konoff, an elderly Russian who had made a fortune manufac-turing zippers. After showing me his factory in Newark (every department was festooned with six-foot zippers for remains bags) he took me back to New York in his chauffeur-driven Cadillac. I noticed that he was holding a copy of *The New Republic,* a magazine read by rather few clients.

"Are you a Democrat or a Republican?" I asked.

"I am a Socialist. I played an active part in the Russian Revolution."

I asked if he had known Kerensky.

"Not *that* revolution," Konoff snorted. "The revolution of 1904. When I was a boy I used to walk five miles to work in a cigarette factory, barefoot in the snow. My real name is Kaganovitch. The FBI thinks that I am the brother of the Kaganovitch who is now in the Politburo. They are mistaken." He roared with laughter. "When I first came to America I worked as a machinist in Pittsburgh for fifty cents an hour. My wife was an embroiderer. She made fourteen dollars a week, but never got paid."

This proud old Socialist millionaire went on to tell me that he had known Lenin and Trotsky intimately during the days of their exile. I listened, so we got the account.

Silence can be golden. Not long ago the advertising manager of Ampex came to see me, scouting for a new agency. For once in my life, I had lunched too well, and had lost the power of speech. All I could do was to motion the prospective client to a seat, and look at him in a questioning way. He talked for an hour, without interruption from me. I could see that he was impressed by my thoughtfulness; it isn't every advertising agent who is so taciturn on these occasions. Then, to my horror, he asked me a question. Had I ever *heard* an Ampex record player? I shook my head, too potted for speech.

"Well, I want you to hear our equipment in your home. It comes in different styles. How is your home decorated?"

I shrugged my shoulders, not trusting myself to speak.

"Modern?"

I shook my head; strong silent man.

"Early American?"

Again I shook my head; still waters run deep.

"Eighteenth century?"

I nodded pensively, but held my tongue. A week later the Ampex arrived. It was magnificent, but my partners decided that the account was too small to be profitable, and I was obliged to withdraw.

Handling accounts once you have got them is deadly serious business. You are spending other people's money, and the fate of their company often rests in your hands. But I regard the hunt for new clients as a *sport* . . . If you play it grimly, you will die of ulcers. If you play it with lighthearted gusto, you will survive your failures without losing sleep. Play to win, but enjoy the fun.

In my youth I sold kitchen stoves at the Ideal Homes Exhibition in London. Each sale required a personalized pitch which took me forty minutes to administer. The problem was to pick out from the milling crowds those rare individuals who were rich enough to buy my stove, which cost $400. I learned to *smell* them; they smoked Turkish cigarettes, a mark of aristocracy, like an Old Etonian tie.

In later years I developed similar techniques for smelling out big advertisers in a crowd. Once I came away from a New York luncheon of the Scottish Council with the presentiment that four of the men I had just met for the first time would one day become my clients. And so it turned out.

*

The biggest account I have ever got was Shell. The Shell people liked what we had done for Rolls-Royce well enough to include us on a list of agencies which they were considering. To each agency they sent a long and searching questionnaire.

Now it so happens that I deplore the practice of selecting agencies by questionnaire, and I have consigned dozens of them to garbage cans. When a company called Stahl-Meyer sent me a question-naire, I replied, "Who is Stahl-Meyer?" But I stayed up all night drafting answers to the Shell questionnaire. My answers were more candid than is customary, but I thought they would make a favor-able impression on Max Burns, a fellow director of the New York

Philharmonic who was then President of Shell, if only they were passed up to him. The next morning I learned that he had gone to England, so I flew to London and left a message at his hotel, saying that I wanted to see him. For ten days there was no reply. I had almost given up hope, when my telephone operator reported that Mr. Burns wanted me to lunch with him on the following day. I had already engaged myself to lunch with the Secretary of State for Scotland, so I sent Burns the following signal:

> Mr. Ogilvy is lunching with the Secretary of State for Scotland at the House of Commons. They would be delighted if you would join them.

On the way to the House – it was pouring rain and we shared an umbrella – I was able to give Burns the gist of my answers to his questionnaire. Back in New York the next day, he introduced me to the man who was about to succeed him as President of Shell – the remarkable Dr. Monroe Spaght. Three weeks later Monty Spaght telephoned to say that we had the account. I was so dumfounded by this momentous news that my aplomb deserted me, and I could only blurt out, "God help us."

Our appointment by Shell forced us to leave the service of Standard Oil (New Jersey). I liked the Jersey people, and I was proud of the part we had played in persuading them to save the superb *Play of the Week* program on television. David Susskind said in *Life* that "if there were a Congressional Medal of Honor for business, this sponsor should get it." But it was not generally known that in order to secure the sponsorship of that program for Jersey, I had been obliged to surrender all my 15 per cent commission to Lorillard, the manufacturers of Old Gold and Kent cigarettes. Lorillard had pre-empted one spot on the doomed program, and only my offer to give them my commission ($6,000 a week) persuaded them to make room for Jersey. I was disappointed with Jersey for refusing to make good my sacrifice. No agency can afford to work without pay; so I transferred my allegiance to Shell.

Sometimes I have made disastrous bloopers in the pursuit of new business. When I met Sir Alexander H. Maxwell, head of the British Travel & Holidays Association, we needed a new account in a hurry. He snubbed me at the start. "Our advertising," he said, "is good, very good indeed. I haven't the remotest intention of changing agencies."

I replied, "When Henry VIII was dying, it was believed that any man who dared to tell him the awful truth would be decapitated. But reasons of state required that a volunteer should be found, and Henry Denny stepped forward. King Henry was so grateful to Denny for his courage that he gave him a pair of gloves and a knighthood. Sir Henry Denny was my ancestor. His example inspires me to tell you that *your advertising is very bad.*"

Maxwell exploded, and never spoke to me again. But shortly afterward he gave us the British Travel account, on condition that I play no part in it, and for many years my partners had to conceal the fact that I was in charge. Our campaign was so successful that the number of American visitors going to Britain quadrupled in ten years. Today Britain earns more from its visitors than any other European country except Italy. "For a small and damp island this is a pretty staggering success," says *The Economist.*

In due course Sir Alexander Maxwell retired, and I was able to come out of hiding. The man who now sits in his chair is Lord Mabane, a former cabinet minister. When I go to England he sends his car to drive me down to Rye, where he lives in Henry James's house. His chauffeur once startled my American wife by asking her if she would like to suck one of his *gums.**

English clients employ rum retainers. The butler at the Rolls-Royce guest house near Derby entered our bedroom on a hot summer morning, without knocking. There lay my wife, sound asleep. Poking his moon face into her ear, he shouted, "Poached or fried, madam?"

Our solicitation of the Armstrong Cork account took a bizarre course. At the start I was bidden to lunch with Max Banzhaf, the advertising manager, at his golf club near Lancaster, Pennsylvania. Our table looked out on the eighteenth green, and for two hours Max regaled me with golfing stories. His assessment of advertising agents appeared to revolve around their ability to hit golf balls. Did I share his love of golf?

I have never been on a golf course in my life, but to admit it at that moment would have destroyed my chances of landing the account. So I mumbled an ambiguous evasion, to the effect that I had no time for games. Max suggested that we play a round, then and there. I protested that I had not brought my clubs.

"I will lend you mine!"

But Max gracefully accepted the next excuse I offered, which had to do with my digestion. And before I left he explained that the only remaining impediment to the success of my solicitation lay in the fact that Henning Prentis, his Chairman, was a devoted and

* English; a goody manufactured by Rowntree.

lifelong friend of Bruce Barton, whose agency had enjoyed a monopoly on Armstrong advertising for forty years.

The following day luck intervened on my side. The Donegal Society invited me to address their annual reunion in one of the oldest Presbyterian churches in the United States. I was to speak from the pulpit, and Mr. Prentis was to be in the congregation. My sermon was fixed for June 23, that marvelous midsummer day on which my grandfather, my father, and I were born.* As my subject I took the role of my fellow countrymen in building America, without referring *directly* to the one Scotsman on Madison Avenue:

> Ralph Waldo Emerson and Thomas Carlyle once went for a walk through the Scottish countryside. When Emerson saw the poor soil around Ecclefechan, he asked Carlyle, "What do you raise on land like this?"
>
> Carlyle replied, "We raise *men*."
>
> What manner of men do they raise on that poor Scottish soil? And what becomes of them when they come to the United States?
>
> They work hard. I was brought up with my father's favorite proverb ringing in my ears, "Hard work never killed a man."
>
> Patrick Henry was a Scot, and John Paul Jones was the son of a Scottish gardener. Allan Pinkerton came from Scotland and

---

* My father once gave me odds of 100 to 1 against my continuing this remarkable series. I haven't yet.

started the secret service. It was Pinkerton who uncovered the first plot to assassinate Lincoln in February 1861.

Thirty-five Justices of the United States Supreme Court have been Scotsmen. And industrialists galore, including an industrialist who has contributed so much to the prosperity and culture of your own Lancaster County – *Mr. Henning Prentis of the Armstrong Cork Company.*

From my vantage point in the pulpit I was able to observe Mr. Prentis' reaction to this apostrophe. He did not look displeased, and a few weeks later he agreed to transfer part of the Armstrong account to our agency.

Of all the new business hoe-downs in which I have engaged, the one with the largest number of contestants was the United States Travel Service. No less than 137 agencies threw their hats into the ring. Our campaigns for Britain and Puerto Rico had been so successful that we were uniquely qualified to advertise the United States as a tourist destination. I longed to infect my fellow Europeans with my own passion for the United States. I had spent my life advertising toothpaste and margarine; what a welcome change it would be to advertise the United States.

Many of the agencies which competed for the account were able to bring political influence to bear; I had none. Nevertheless we got on the short list of six, and were invited to make a presentation in Washington. Assistant Secretary of Commerce William Ruder – in private life a fellow denizen of Madison Avenue – subjected me to a merciless cross-examination which exposed the one weakness in my case: a lack of branch offices in foreign countries.

After making more than a hundred new-business presentations, I have come to know by the end of the meeting whether I have won or lost. That afternoon I knew that I had lost, and I returned to New York in despair. Ten days went by, and no announcement was made. I was comforted by my staff, and we laid bets on which of our competitors would win. Then one Saturday morning I was awakened by Western Union: the Secretary of Commerce had appointed Ogilvy, Benson & Mather to do the "Visit U.S.A." advertising in Britain, France, and Germany.

This was the most glorious telegram I had received since Oxford telegraphed the news of my scholarship at Christ Church thirty years before. Every advertisement I write for the U. S. Travel Service is a bread-and-butter letter from a grateful immigrant.

Before our campaign broke I warned the Department of Commerce that it was bound to attract criticism:

> The crunch will come when our first advertisement appears. *Whatever* the advertisements say or don't say, we are going to be subjected to criticism. I know this from long experience with the British travel advertising.

> But in the last analysis, our campaign can only be defended or attacked on the basis of *results*.

Research had revealed that our greatest single obstacle lay in the fact that Europeans had an exaggerated concept of the cost of visiting the U.S.A. We decided to attack the problem head-on. Instead of saying in a bland, innocuous way that you can tour America "for less than you suppose," we gave a specific figure: £35 a week. This was arrived at after careful verification. For example, before deciding on a reasonable minimum price for a hotel room in New York, we sent one of our copywriters to check the beds at the Hotel Winslow, which charges six dollars a night; she found them satisfactory.

But our critics took the position that £35 a week was far too low. They were not aware of the realities of the problem:

(1) Travel from Europe had previously been confined to businessmen with expense accounts, and the very rich. It was vitally important to enlarge the market by attracting tourists with more modest means. Fort Knox was leaking gold, and foreign exchange was urgently needed.

(2) Whereas more than half the families in the United States have incomes in excess of $5,000 only *3 per cent* of the families in England have incomes of this magnitude. It was therefore important to make our product available to them at the lowest possible price; they could always spend more if they wanted to.

(3) It is better, I argued, for middle-income Europeans to visit the United States even if they have to economize than not to come at all; the thrill of seeing New York, San Francisco, and the wide-open spaces far transcends any hardships involved in economizing. Foreign tourists bring badly needed foreign exchange, and research shows that almost all of them go home with a more favorable attitude toward the United States.

Our advertisements achieved record-breaking readership when they appeared in European newspapers, and they produced so many inquiries that the London, Paris, and Frankfurt offices of the U. S. Travel Service had to work far into the night.

Our campaign triggered an avalanche of editorial publicity which was probably without precedent in the history of advertising. *The Daily Mail* sent its star feature writer to the United States. In his first dispatch he cabled:

> At the same time as President Kennedy invited me – and all the other millions of Europe – to try the novelty of tourism in the U.S., he issued a secret directive to 180,000,000 Americans to be nice to us. How else to explain the embarrassing generosity, the overwhelming kindness, the extreme courtesy at every turn?

The Daily Express instructed its New York correspondent to write a series of articles on the subject. An editorial in *The Manchester Guardian* referred to our advertisements as "famous," after only three of them had appeared. *Handelsblatt*, the leading financial newspaper in Germany, wrote: "This is a very *truthful* campaign. The U. S. Travel Service has introduced its advertising to the West German tourist market with a blare of trumpets."

The proof of the pudding is in the eating. Eight months after our campaign started, French tourist traffic to the United States was up 27 per cent, British traffic was up 24 per cent, and German traffic was up 18 per cent.

In 1956 I participated in an unusual adventure: a joint solicitation with another agency. Ben Sonnenberg persuaded Arthur Fatt of Grey and myself to solicit the Greyhound Bus account – in tandem. He specified that I was to "upgrade the image of bus travel," while Grey was to "put arses on the seats."

Fatt and I flew to San Francisco, where the Greyhound people were holding a convention. As soon as we had checked into our hotel, he showed me his presentation. His research department had penetrated to the heart of the problem, and his copywriters had developed a slogan which hit the nail on the head – *It's such a comfort to take the bus and leave the driving to us.*

Forthwith I called the Greyhound advertising manager on the house phone, and invited him to join me in Fatt's room.

"Arthur Fatt has just shown me his half of our joint presentation. It is the best I have ever seen. I advise you to give your *whole* account to Grey. To make your decision easier, I am now returning to New York."

I then left the room, and Grey was appointed.

I have never wanted to get an account so big that I could not afford to lose it. The day you do that, you commit yourself to living with fear. Frightened agencies lose the courage to give candid advice; once you lose that you become a lackey.

This was what led me to refuse an invitation to compete for the Edsel account. I wrote to Ford: "Your account would represent one-half of our total billing. This would make it difficult for us to sustain our independence of counsel." If we had entered the Edsel contest, and if we had won it, Ogilvy, Benson & Mather would have gone down the drain with Edsel.

We take immense pains to select our clients. It is true that we have selected a few clients who have not yet selected us, but we persevere in their pursuit, and we turn down an average of fifty-nine less desirable accounts every year.

It is not generally realized that there aren't enough first-class agencies to go around. For example, when the soap manufacturers have roped off their twenty-one agencies, there are only two left which could meet their standards.

My ambition is to add one new client every two years. Faster growth would force us to engage new staff faster than we could train them, and to divert too much of our best brain power from the service of our old clients to the difficult work involved in planning the first campaigns for new ones. I seek accounts which meet ten criteria:

(1) The product must be one which we would be proud to advertise. On those few occasions when we have advertised products which we privately despised, we have failed. A lawyer may be able to defend a murderer whom he knows to be guilty, and a surgeon may be able to operate on a man he dislikes, but professional detachment doesn't work in advertising. Some measure of personal commitment is required before a copywriter can sell a product.

(2) I never accept an account unless I believe that we can do a conspicuously better job than the previous agency. When *The New York Times* asked us to do their advertising, I declined, because I didn't think we could produce better advertisements than the brilliant ones they had been running.

(3) I steer clear of products whose sales have been falling over a long period, because this almost always means that there is an intrinsic weakness in the product, or that the management of the company is incompetent. No amount of good advertising can make up for either of these deficiencies.

However hungry a new agency may be, it must have the self-restraint to turn down moribund accounts. A surgeon with an established practice can afford to have an occasional patient die on the operating table, but a young surgeon's whole career can be ruined by such a misadventure. I used to dread having one of our accounts die on our operating table.

(4) It is important to find out whether the prospective client wants his agency to make a profit. I have had the galling experience of helping to make clients into multimillionaires while losing my shirt in their service. The average profit made by advertising agencies is now less than half of one per cent. We tread a narrow knife-edge, poised between overservicing our clients and going broke, or underservicing them and getting fired.

(5) If the account is unlikely to be profitable, would it give you a chance to create remarkable advertising? We never made much profit on Guinness or Rolls-Royce, but they gave us golden opportunities to demonstrate our creative excellence. There is no quicker way to put a new agency on the map. The only danger is that it gives you a lopsided reputation. The business world assumes that if a small agency demonstrates a genius for creating great advertisements, it must be weak in research and marketing. It seldom occurs to people that if you set high standards in one department, you are likely to set high standards in every department.

(I myself was soon type-cast as a good copywriter, but an ignoramus in every other department. This irritated me, because my long suit was not copy at all, but research; I had run the Audience Research Institute for Dr. Gallup.

The biggest problem which besets almost every agency is the problem of producing good campaigns. Copywriters, art directors, and television producers are easily come by, but the number of men who can preside over an agency's entire creative output – perhaps a hundred new campaigns every year – can be numbered on the fingers of one hand. These rare trumpeter swans must be capable of inspiring a motley crew of writers and artists; they must be sure-footed judges of campaigns for a wide range of different products; they must be good presenters; and they must have a colossal appetite for midnight oil.

Word got around that I was one of these rare birds, and it occurred to several of the big agencies that they should hire me, even if they had to take my whole agency to get me. In a period of three years I received such offers from J. Walter Thompson, McCann-Erickson, BBDO, Leo Burnett, and five other agencies. If it had occurred to any of them to woo me with *gold*, I would have succumbed. But they all made the mistake of assuming that I was more interested in "creative challenge," whatever that may be.)

A lopsided reputation for creativity disqualifies an agency from getting big accounts. But it is something you must risk if you are ever going to escape from obscurity. It wasn't until Esty Stowell joined us in 1957 that our agency began to acquire a reputation for strength in *all* departments. He had been Executive Vice President of Benton & Bowles, which was widely regarded as the best of all agencies in the marketing area. He was the symbol we required to offset my reputation as a mere copywriter; he was also a very able man. With a sigh of relief I turned over to him the management of every department in the agency except the creative departments. From that point on our agency began to grow in bigger chunks.

(6) The relationship between a manufacturer and his advertising agency is almost as intimate as the relationship between a patient and his doctor. Make sure that you can live happily with your prospective client before you accept his account.

When a prospective client comes to see me for the first time, I start by finding out why he wants to change agencies. If I have reason to suspect that he has been resigned, I ask a friend in his previous agency. Only recently I discovered in the nick of time that a prospective client had been resigned; his previous agency told me that he needed a psychiatrist more than an agency.

(7) I avoid clients for whom advertising is only a marginal factor in their marketing mix. They have an awkward tendency to raid their advertising appropriations whenever they need cash for other purposes. I prefer clients for whom advertising is the breath of life. We then find ourselves operating at the indispensable heart of our client's business, instead of on the frivolous fringe.

On the whole, the most lucrative accounts are products of low unit cost, universal use, and frequent purchase. They generate larger budgets, and more opportunities for testing, than high-priced durables.

(8) I never take *new* products, before they have emerged from the laboratory, unless they are included in a hamper with another product which has already reached national distribution. It costs an agency more to steer a new product through test markets than to handle a going product, and eight out of ten new products die in test markets. With an over-all profit margin of *one-half of one per cent*, we cannot afford this risk.

(9) If you aspire to produce great advertising, never take *associations* as clients. Some years ago, we were invited to compete for the Rayon Manufacturers' Association account. I duly presented myself at their headquarters and was ushered into a pompous committee room.

"Mr. Ogilvy," said the chairman, "we are interviewing several agencies. You have exactly fifteen minutes to plead your case. Then I will *ring this bell*, and the representative of the next agency, who is already waiting outside, will follow you."

Before launching into my pitch, I asked three questions:

"How many of the end-uses for rayon must be covered in your campaign?" Answer: automobile tires, furnishing fabrics, industrial products, women's clothing, men's clothing.

"How much money is available?" Answer: $600,000.

"How many people must OK the advertisements?" Answer: the twelve members of the Committee, representing twelve manufacturers.

"Ring the bell!" I said, and walked out.

Them's the conditions what prevail with almost all association accounts. Too many masters, too many objectives, too little money.

(10) Sometimes a prospective client offers you business on condition that you hire an individual whom he believes to be indispensable to the management of his advertising. The agencies which play this game wind up with a crew of politicians who cock snooks

at their plans board, ignore their copy chief, and blackmail their management. I have sometimes hired able men on condition that they did not bring their vest-pocket accounts with them.

However thoroughly you investigate prospective clients, it is almost impossible to find out whether they qualify on all these counts *until you meet them face to face* . . . You then find yourself in a delicate position, simultaneously selling your agency and eliciting from the prospect enough information about himself and his product to decide whether you want his account. It pays to listen more than you talk.

In early days I sometimes made the mistake of not exhibiting sufficient enthusiasm for the account I was soliciting. My style was too diffident. Thus when Ted Moscoso, the brilliant head of Puerto Rico's Operation Bootstrap, first came to see me, he went away with the impression that it was a matter of indifference to me whether he hired us or not. It took me a long time to convince him that I really wanted to work for Puerto Rico.

Shortly after our appointment as the agency for Puerto Rico, I wrote to Moscoso:

We must substitute a *lovely* image of Puerto Rico for the squalid image which now exists in the minds of most mainlanders. This is of cardinal importance to your industrial development, your rum industry, your tourism and your political evolution.

What *is* Puerto Rico? What is the personality of this island? What face shall Puerto Rico show to the world? Is Puerto Rico no more than a backward country in the throes of its industrial revolution? Is the island to remain what Max Ascoli calls "the Formosa of the

New Dealers"? Is it in the process of becoming a latterday North Philadelphia? Or is there a soul alive in the body economic?

Is Puerto Rico to be overrun by vulgar tourists, and changed into a second-class Miami Beach? Have Puerto Ricans forgotten their Spanish heritage in a mad rush to prove how American they are?

These imminent tragedies need not be. And one of the surest ways to prevent them is to start a long-range advertising campaign that will present Puerto Rico to the world in the image which inspires us all – an image of Puerto Rico in renaissance.

Ted Moscoso and Governor Muñoz accepted this proposal, and we launched the campaign which is still running, nine years later. It has had a profound effect on the fortunes of Puerto Rico. It is, I believe, the only instance of an advertising campaign changing the image of a country.

One day in 1959, Moscoso and I were lunching with Beardsley Ruml and Elmo Roper at the Century. Walking me back to my office, Moscoso said, "David, you've been doing our Puerto Rico advertising for five years. This afternoon I'm going to telephone all your other clients and invite them to join me in a proposition: if you will stop soliciting new clients, we will promise never to fire you. Wouldn't you like to devote all your energy to the clients you already have, and stop wasting your time in the pursuit of new ones?"

I was sorely tempted to encourage this novel proposal. Landing new clients is exciting, but each one increases my load of home-work; eighty hours a week are enough. But my younger partners were hungry for new challenges. What's more, even the best agencies lose accounts. Sometimes it happens that clients sell their companies; sometimes they hire bullies to manage their advertising, and I always resign from the service of bullies. So, if you stop adding new clients, you start bleeding to death. (But this doesn't mean that you have to follow Ben Duffy's example. When he was head of BBDO he took every new account that was offered, and wound up with 167; the pressure almost killed him. Stanley Resor was the opposite. In his first year as head of J. Walter Thompson he resigned a hundred accounts, unprofitable undergrowth. That was his first step in making JWT the biggest agency in the world.)

A posture of enthusiasm is not *always* the one best calculated to succeed. Five or six times I have turned down accounts which did not meet our qualifications, only to find that the act of rejection inflamed the client's desire to hire our agency. When a famous Swiss watch manufacturer offered us his account, we declined, because his advertisements had to be approved not only by headquarters in Switzerland but also by the American importer, and no advertising agent can serve two masters. But instead of declining in a straightforward way, I said that we would accept the account if we were paid 25 per cent instead of the usual 15 per cent commission. The client promptly agreed.

Sometimes a manufacturer in search of a new agency releases to the newspapers the names of the agencies he is considering. Whenever we are revealed as one of the suitors, I withdraw from the contest; it is unwise to risk being *publicly* defeated. I like to succeed in public, but to fail in secret.

I avoid contests in which more than four other agencies are involved. The ritual of competitive courtship requires a series of long meetings. A hot agency finds itself on the shopping list of almost every prospective client, and it is all too easy for its top man to fritter away his time in this way. We have other fish to fry – the fish of our present clients.

The most desirable courtship is the kind which involves no other agency. This is becoming increasingly rare, because corporate men now seem to think it naughty to hire a new agency without comparing the merits of several. In Chapter IV I will offer them free advice on the right way to go about selecting a new agency.

Most agencies send large delegations to present their case to prospective clients. The head of the agency limits his own participation to introducing a series of subordinates, who take turns haranguing the prospect. I have always preferred to make the presentation myself. The final choice of agency is almost always made by the head of the client company, and chairmen should be harangued by chairmen.

I have also found that frequent changes of speaker lead to confusion with the other agencies which are competing for the account. One orchestra looks like every other orchestra, but there is no confusing one conductor with another. When we were invited to solicit the Sears, Roebuck account I bearded their board of directors by myself. Sophisticated corporations are seldom deceived by a show of bodies. The agencies with the best record in new-business solicitation rely on their leader to put on solo performances. (When you consider the repulsive personalities of many of these soloists, you are forced to conclude that *singularity* is an important ingredient in winning accounts.)

I always tell prospective clients about the chinks in our armor. I have noticed that when an antique dealer draws my attention to flaws in a piece of furniture, he wins my confidence.

What *are* the chinks in our armor? The two most important are
these:

> We have no Public Relations department. I take the view that
> public relations should be handled by the manufacturer
> himself, or by specialist counsel.

> We have never produced a television spectacular. I have a
> phobia for these extravaganzas; with rare exceptions they cost
> too much in relation to the size of the audience they deliver.

Try as I may, I have never been able to space the acquisition of new
accounts at convenient intervals. For months on end, nothing
happens. I begin to wonder if we will *ever* get another account. My
staff becomes despondent. Then we get three beauties in rapid
succession, and the load of urgent work becomes unbearable. The
only solution is to build a waiting list of would-be clients, and to
admit them one by one at times of our own choosing. That will be
the day.

III How to Keep Clients

The seven-year itch is not confined to matrimony. It also afflicts the relationship between advertising agents and their clients. The average client changes agencies once every seven years. He gets *bored* with his agency, much as a gourmet gets bored with the repertoire of his chef.

Winning a new account is a heady experience, but losing one is pure hell. What do you do to convince your other clients that they too should not dismiss you? I have seen two large agencies collapse after one defecting client started a run on the bank; it is a sickening spectacle.

What does the agency president do about his conscience when he knows that it was his own fault that his agency lost the account? How can he, in common decency, fire the people who worked on the account and did their best to offset his own stupidity? Some of them may be men of rare ability, and he will need them to work on the next new account he brings in. But can he afford to keep them on ice? Generally not. I have seen agencies fire a hundred people when they have lost a single account; and some of those poor devils were too old to get another job. This is one reason why agencies have to pay such high salaries; next to the theater, advertising is probably the least secure of all careers.

If you aspire to manage an agency, you must accept the fact that you are always going to be traveling on the edge of a precipice. If you are naturally an insecure, frightened person, woe betide you. You are in for a rough passage.

I envy my friends who are doctors. They have so many patients that the defection of one cannot ruin them. Nor is the defection reported in the newspapers for all their other patients to read.

I also envy lawyers. They can go on their vacations, safe in the knowledge that other lawyers are not making love to their clients. Now that I have acquired a portfolio of nineteen splendid clients, I wish that a law could be passed making it illegal for agencies to solicit. In Sweden the big agencies have got such a law onto the statute books, in delightful restraint of trade.

There are certain steps you can take to reduce the turnover. First and foremost, you can devote your best brains to the service of your clients, instead of diverting them to the pursuit of new ones. I have always forbidden my account executives to hunt new clients, because it corrupts them, like playing the horses. They start neglecting their present clients, and the revolving door starts spinning.

Second, you can avoid hiring unstable, quarrelsome executives. Madison Avenue is full of masochists who unconsciously provoke rejection by their clients. I know brilliant men who have lost every account they have ever handled. And I know pedestrian nonentities who have a genius for creating relationships of calm stability between the agency and its clients.

Third, you can avoid taking on clients who have a record of firing their agencies at frequent intervals. You may think that you can cure them of their infidelity, but the odds are against you, as they are when you marry a much-divorced woman.

Fourth, you can keep in contact with your clients *at all their levels*. But this is becoming increasingly difficult as the big advertisers pile level upon level – assistant brand managers reporting to brand managers, reporting to division heads, reporting to marketing vice presidents, reporting to executive vice presidents, reporting to presidents, reporting to chairmen – with a battery of consultants, committees, and staff officers heckling the agency from the wings. It has become the fashion for most corporate chairmen and presidents to insulate themselves from all contact with their agencies. Mind you, they still make the important decisions with respect to their advertising, but they never see the agency people face to face, and their henchmen are often incompetent to serve as go-betweens. Frequently I hear advertising managers quote their presidents as uttering stupidities which I know they could never have said. And I have no doubt that these same presidents hear me quoted as saying some pretty silly things. Before you know it, you are fired.

It reminds me of a story told during the First World War. A brigade major sent a verbal message back from the front-line trench to his divisional headquarters. The message started out as *"Send up reinforcements, we are going to advance."* By the time it had been repeated from mouth to mouth through all the levels, it reached headquarters as *"Send up three-and-four-pence, we are going to a dance."*

One of the reasons why the top people in big corporations show this tendency to deal with agencies at arm's length is that they dislike the whole business of advertising. It is so intangible. When they build new factories, or issue new stock, or buy raw materials, they know exactly what they are getting. These propositions are presented to them cut-and-dried, with all the facts and figures they need to justify their decision to their stockholders. But advertising is still an inexact speculation. As the first Lord Leverhulme (and John Wanamaker after him) complained, "Half the money I spend on advertising is wasted, and the trouble is I don't know which half."

Manufacturers who have come up through production or accounting or research are apt to be suspicious of advertising people, because they are too articulate. That is why some inarticulate dullards have done so well as the heads of agencies: they make their clients feel comfortable.

Another thing you can do to reduce the risk of losing accounts is to adopt my *ice-box policy*. As soon as a client has approved a new campaign, begin work to develop another one, and put it in test markets. You will then be ready with a shot in your locker if your first campaign flops, or incurs the displeasure of your client's top management for some more subjective reason. This restless preparation of reserve positions will cut into your profits and exasperate your copywriters, but it will prolong your tenure of accounts.

I have always tried to sit on the same side of the table as my clients, to see problems through their eyes. I buy shares in their company, so that I can think like a member of their family. When I take a *total* view of their business, I am better able to give them sound advice. If they would elect me to their board of directors, it would be even easier to identify myself with their best interests.

Young eager beavers often have the bright idea of combining two of their clients in a joint operation. They may suggest that one client should mount a contest and offer another client's product as the prize; or that two clients should share an advertisement in magazines. This doubling-up can be dangerous to the agency; almost invariably one of the clients will feel that he has got the short end of the stick. When you try to umpire disputes between clients, you end up with a bloody nose. I was brought up to keep my clients apart. The only time the head of Hathaway met the head of Schweppes was when they went to buy a Rolls-Royce on the same morning.

I never tell one client that I cannot attend his sales convention because I have a previous engagement with another client; successful polygamy depends upon pretending to each spouse that she is the only pebble on your beach. If one client asks me what results I have been getting with a campaign for another client, I change the subject. This may irritate him, but if I were to give him the information he asks, he would probably conclude that I would be equally indiscreet with *his* secrets. Once a client loses confidence in your discretion, you've had it.

Sometimes a client hires an advertising manager who is so incompetent that you have to denounce him. But I have only done this twice in fifteen years. In one case the man was a psychotic whom I had fired six months before. In the other case he was a pathological liar.

Most reasonable clients seem to regard it as your duty to alert them when you detect a weak link in the chain of communication between their top management and yours. I was once taken to task by a client for not warning him that our account executive was ghosting his brand manager's marketing plans.

Clients do not hesitate to blackball our account executives. Sometimes they are right; sometimes they are wrong. In either case it is better for all concerned to transfer the victim to another job, and to do it before the smoke bursts into flame and ruptures the whole agency-client relationship.

One of the most brilliant colleagues I ever had was blackballed by three clients in one year; the experience hurt him so badly that he left the agency business forever. If you are too thin-skinned to survive this hazard, you should not become an account executive in an advertising agency.

I always use my clients' products. This is not toadyism, but elementary good manners. Almost everything I consume is manufactured by one of my clients. My shirts are by Hathaway, my candlesticks by Steuben. My car is a Rolls-Royce, and its tank is always full of Super Shell. I have my suits made by Sears, Roebuck. At breakfast I drink Maxwell House coffee or Tetley Tea, and eat two slices of Pepperidge Farm toast. I wash with Dove, deodorize with Ban, and light my pipe with a Zippo lighter. After sundown I drink nothing but Puerto Rico rum and Schweppes. I read magazines and newspapers which are printed on paper from the mills of International Paper. When I go on vacation (in Britain or Puerto Rico) I get my reservations through American Express and travel by KLM or P&O-Orient Lines.

And why not, pray tell? Are these not the finest goods and services on earth? I think they are, and that is why I advertise them.

When a client hires our agency, it is because he has decided that it is the best available to him. His advisers have reached this decision after making a thorough study of what we have to offer. But as time goes by, he acquires new advisers. Every time this happens, it is expedient for the agency to convince the new adviser that his predecessor was right in selecting our agency. The new adviser should be treated as if he were a new business prospect.

With big corporations, this process of reselling the agency never

ends. It is time-consuming and wearisome, but it is vitally important. New brooms are a constant threat to the stability of agency-
client relationships.

The most dangerous thing that can happen to an agency is to
depend on a single personal tie with a client company. If the president of a large manufacturing organization hires your agency
because he likes your president, you must take urgent steps to
forge ties at lower levels. Only when the agency is wired in at *every*
level can you hope for tenure.

I do not believe in restricting contact with the client to the account
executives. It works better to have people from your service departments – research, media, copy, art, television production,
merchandising, and so on – get to know your client. This sometimes presents comic problems, because our backroom boys are
not always remarkable for their tact, and some of them are unim-
pressive in their persons. It takes a client of rare perception to
recognize that a tongue-tied hobbledehoy may be capable of
writing a commercial which will double his sales.

It is difficult for a doctor to tell a patient that he is suffering from
a serious disease, and it is equally difficult to tell a client that his
product has a serious fault. I have known clients who resent such
candor more than they would resent criticism of their wives. A
manufacturer's pride in his product almost always blinds him to its
shortcomings. But the time comes in the life of every advertising
agent when he must grasp this nettle. I confess that I am no good
at it. When I told one client that I had doubts about the consis-
tency of his spaghetti, his reaction was to question whether I could
do a good job for any product which I disliked; we lost the
account. On the whole, however, I have observed an increasing

tendency on the part of clients to welcome candor, particularly when it is based on the results of consumer research.

The head of an agency has so much on his plate that he is apt to see his clients only at times of crisis. This is a mistake. If you get into the habit of seeing clients when the weather is calm, you will establish an easy relationship which may save your life when a storm blows up.

It is important to admit your mistakes, and to do so before you are charged with them. Many clients are surrounded by buckpassers who make a fine art of blaming the agency for their own failures. I seize the earliest opportunity to assume the blame.

Come to think of it, we have resigned three times as many clients as we have been fired by. I will not allow my staff to be bullied by tyrants, and I will not run a campaign dictated by a client unless I believe in its basic soundness. When you do that, you imperil the creative reputation of your agency, which ought to be your most treasured possession. In 1954 I made this very mistake. My friend Jerry Babb at Lever Brothers was insisting that we advertise the old Rinso soap powder and the new Rinso Blue detergent in the same advertisements. A study of the precedents had taught me that it doesn't pay to advertise two products in one advertisement, particularly when one of them is new and the other is obsolescent. Even worse, Jerry instructed me to inject a note of whimsical gaiety into the campaign.

For several weeks I tried to sell him the kind of serious campaign which had proved successful for Tide and other detergents, but Jerry was adamant. Storm signals were hoisted. His right-hand man warned me that unless I did as I was told, I would lose the account. In the end, I capitulated. It took me two hours and a pint of Puerto

Rican rum to write the silliest copy in the history of advertising. It was in verse, to be sung to the tune of "Boys and Girls Come Out to Play":

> Rinso White or Rinso Blue?
> Soap or detergent – it's up to you!
> Both wash whiter and brighter than new,
> The choice, dear lady, is up to *you*!

This dreadful doggerel duly appeared. I lost more face than I could afford; my staff thought that I had gone mad, and the working levels at Lever Brothers concluded that I had no conception of what kind of advertising was required to persuade housewives to buy a detergent. Six months later we were fired, and deserved to be.

Nor did the mischief end there. For several years afterward I found it impossible to get any serious marketing man to join Ogilvy, Benson & Mather until I had told him that my opinion of my idiotic Rinso campaign was as low as his own.

This episode taught me that it does not pay to appease clients on matters of grand strategy. One Munich was enough.

I also resign accounts when they are unprofitable to my agency. This happened with Reed & Barton. Our commissions were not big enough to pay for the services which were required, and Roger Hallowell, who managed this fine old family business, was unwilling to make good the losses we were incurring. I liked Roger and all his colleagues at Reed & Barton, but I was not prepared to trade with them indefinitely at a loss. I believe that they made a mistake in allowing us to resign; we had made an important contribution to their profits by showing them how to pretest new patterns for sterling flatware. It costs $500,000 to launch a new pattern, and no male executive can predict what patterns will appeal to nineteen-year-old brides.

I also resign accounts when I lose confidence in the product. It is flagrantly dishonest for an advertising agent to urge consumers to buy a product which he would not allow his own wife to buy.

Frank Hummert, who succeeded Claude Hopkins as copy chief of Lord & Thomas and then made a fortune as the inventor of soap operas, once told me: "All clients are *pigs* . . . You may start by thinking otherwise, but you will change your mind."

This has not been my experience. I have encountered a handful of pigs and I have resigned them. But with a very few exceptions, I have loved my clients. If I hadn't become his advertising agent, I would never have made friends with Ted Moscoso, the great Puerto Rican who became American Ambassador to Venezuela and head of the Alliance for Progress.

If I hadn't landed the Steuben Glass account, I would never have made friends with Arthur Houghton. It was a great day for me when I realized that I had acquired as a client the foremost patron of contemporary artists in the history of industry, an eminent authority on rare books, and the most imaginative of philanthropists.

My list of clients who became dear friends is a long one. Ellerton Jetté of Hathaway enriched my life by getting me elected to the Board of Trustees at Colby College. Sir Colin Anderson of P&O-Orient Lines is the only client I have ever had who is equally expert at Scottish dancing and embroidery. Commander Whitehead of Schweppes started out as a client and became one of my closest companions. We have been shipwrecked together, and our wives solace each other by comparing notes on their husbands' vanities.

Helena Rubinstein has always fascinated me. This tiny Polish beauty started her career in Australia in the nineteenth century, and made a profit of £30,000 when she was eighteen years old. By the time she discovered me, she had become a matriarch, in control of companies all over the world. In the office she is a terror, but she also has an irresistible sense of humor. A hundred times I have seen her, in the middle of an otherwise grim meeting, so convulsed by laughter that the tears ran down her cheeks. As a friend, she is an enchanting combination of gaiety and generosity.

Another thing I admire in Madame Rubinstein is her lack of pretense; she is as remarkable as she looks, and no pretense is needed. That is what Graham Sutherland captured in his portrait of her.

Some agencies pander to the craze for doing everything in committee. They boast about "teamwork" and decry the role of the individual. But no *team* can write an advertisement, and I doubt whether there is a single agency of any consequence which is not the lengthened shadow of one man.

Clients sometimes ask me what would become of our agency if I were run over by a taxicab. It would change. When Senator Benton and Governor Bowles left their agency, it changed – for the better. J. Walter Thompson survived the departure of Mr. Thompson. McCann-Erickson hit its stride after Harry McCann retired. Even the retirement of Raymond Rubicam, who was probably the best agency head in history, failed to arrest the progress of Young & Rubicam.

Like a midwife, I make my living bringing new babies into the world, except that mine are new advertising campaigns. Once or twice a week I go into our Delivery Room and preside over what is known as a Presentation. These awesome ceremonies are attended by six or seven of my henchmen and notables from the client's official family. The atmosphere is electric. The client knows that he is going to be asked to approve a campaign which will cost millions. The agency has invested much time and treasure in preparing its offering.

At my agency we always rehearse our presentations before our Plans Board, on which sit our senior senators. They are sterner critics than any client I have so far encountered, and their criticisms are expressed in rougher language. By the time a campaign has passed their scrutiny, it is apt to be good.

But however well-documented our presentation may be, however thoroughly our planners have assessed the marketing realities, and however brilliantly our copywriters have done their work, horrible things can happen at The Presentation. If it begins early in the morning, the client may have a hangover. On one occasion I made the mistake of presenting a new campaign to Sam Bronfman of Seagram after luncheon. He fell sound asleep, and awoke in such a poisonous humor that he rejected the campaign on which we had been working for several months.

Bronfman disliked the convention which most agencies observe of using several spokesmen to make their presentations. So do I. It is less distracting to the audience if one man does all the talking. He should be the most persuasive advocate available, and he should be so thoroughly briefed that he can stand up under cross-examination.

I make more presentations than most agency heads, partly because I fancy myself as an advocate, and partly because I believe that there is no better way of demonstrating to the client that the head of the agency is personally involved in his affairs. I wonder if any barrister has to spend as many nights as I do preparing for the Presentations which succeed each other with such remorseless regularity.

It pays to take immense pains in preparing the plans you present to clients. They should be written with the maximum lucidity and the least possible mannerism. They should be laced with irrefutable facts.

But there are still a few clients who do not like their agencies to present advertisements in the context of a well-documented plan. They enjoy appraising layouts in a vacuum, as if they were selecting pictures for an exhibition. Sir Frederic Hooper of Schweppes belongs to this school. The first time I presented a marketing plan to him, he quickly became bored. He had been looking forward to a diverting half-hour of literary criticism, and found himself being subjected to a tedious recitation of marketing facts. On page 19 of my presentation I came to a statistic that contradicted one of his basic assumptions. "Ogilvy," he thundered, "your statistical approach to advertising is positively *babyish*."

I wondered what effect this compliment would have on the statisticians who had prepared our plan. But I stuck to my guns, and five years later Sir Frederic made an *amende honorable* when he invited me to address an advertising convention over which he was to preside. He suggested that I take as my text a conclusion at which he had recently arrived: "In the end, clients are grateful to advertising agents who tell them the truth." By that time Schweppes' sales in the United States had increased 517 per cent. We lived happily ever after.

Another client who did not want to be confused with facts complained to me with the utmost gravity, "David, the trouble with your agency is that it contains too many people with objective minds."

The best tool ever devised for explaining complicated plans to committees is the flip-over easel, which the presenter reads aloud. It has the effect of riveting the attention of everyone in the room on what you are saying . . . Here I have some advice to offer. It may sound trivial, but it can be crucial to the success of the presentation: *as you read aloud, never depart from your printed text by a single word* . . . The trick lies in assaulting your audience simultaneously through their eyes and their ears. If they see one set of words, and hear a different set, they become confused and inattentive.

I still die a thousand deaths before every presentation. I am particularly nervous about the impact of my English accent.

How can an American manufacturer possibly have any confidence in the ability of a foreigner to influence the behavior of American housewives? In my heart I know that my years with Dr. Gallup at Princeton gave me more insight into the habits and mentality of the American consumer than most native copywriters can bring to bear, and I always hope that this will become apparent as my presentation unfolds. I therefore open with axioms which nobody can question. By the time the audience grows accustomed to my accent, I launch into more controversial judgments.

The first time I allowed a member of my staff to present one of my campaigns to a client, I knew that my presence at the meeting would increase his nervousness. So I concealed myself in the next room and observed his performance through a peephole. His name was Garret Lydecker, and he performed better than I have ever done, before or since.

Nowadays I have several partners who are first-class presenters, and I no longer hesitate to attend their presentations. They have learned to preserve their equanimity, even when I heckle them. In the discussion which follows, we hammer out a position which was neither the client's nor the agency's at the beginning of the meeting. The result is a feeling of comradeship, cutting across the lines which traditionally keep agency and client on opposite sides of the table.

In some agencies the account executives are allowed to boss the creative people. This makes a good impression on some clients; they believe that their advertising is safer in the hands of "business" men. But it creates an atmosphere which inhibits copywriters, and the client winds up with second-rate advertising. In other agencies the account executives are little more than waiters who carry confections from the campaign-builders to the clients. They are forbidden to accept the slightest modification which the client may propose without referring back to headquarters. Denied the authority to exercise their own judgment, they end up as errand boys.

I deplore both systems . . . I have able copywriters, and they work in tandem with able account executives who are empowered to negotiate with clients. The account executives are sufficiently mature to manage every phase of their accounts without challenging the ultimate suzerainty of the copywriter. It is a delicate balance, and I know of only one other agency which has ever achieved it.

The marketing plans coming out of our agency today are more professional, more objective, and better documented than the plans I used to write in our early days. But some of them are written in a business lingo which makes me squirm – percentage-wise, importantly, mitigate against, maximize, and so on. As a boy I was obliged to learn twelve verses of the Bible by heart before breakfast every morning, and I read Latin from the age of nine. At Oxford I came under the influence of dons who rejected the German school of scholarship – dry-as-dust, humorless, and unreadable. I was taught to admire not Mommsen, but Gibbon, Macaulay, and Trevelyan, who wrote to be read. This kind of training did not equip me to read the turgid documents which are my homework today. American businessmen are not taught that it is a sin to *bore* your fellow creatures.

IV How to Be a Good Client

ONE of the biggest advertisers in the world recently engaged an illustrious firm of management engineers to study the relationship between his advertising and his profit. The statistician who made the study fell into a trap which is curiously common: he assumed that the only significant variable was the *amount* of *money* spent on advertising from year to year. He was not aware that a million dollars' worth of effective advertising can sell more than ten million dollars' worth of ineffective advertising.

Mail-order advertisers have found that a mere change of headline can increase sales ten times; and I have seen television commercials sell five times as much of a product as other commercials written by the same man.

I know of a brewer who sells more of his beer to the people who never see his advertising than to the people who see it every week. Bad advertising can *unsell* a product.

Sometimes the responsibility for such catastrophes rests on the agency, but often it is the client who is to blame. Clients get the advertising they deserve. I have worked for ninety-six of them, and have had unique opportunities for comparing their attitudes and procedures. Some behave so badly that no agency could produce effective advertising for them. Some behave so well that no agency could fail to do so.

In this chapter, I will set down the fifteen rules which I would obey in dealing with my agency if I became a client. They are calculated to extract the best service.

(1) *Emancipate your agency from fear.*

Most agencies run scared, most of the time. This is partly because many of the people who gravitate to the agency business are naturally insecure, and partly because many clients make it unmistakably plain that they are always on the lookout for a new agency. Frightened people are powerless to produce good advertising.

After I resigned the Rolls-Royce account, I invited myself to visit the Ford Motor Company, "to get acquainted." To his everlasting credit, the advertising manager of Ford refused to receive me. He said: "Detroit is a small town. If you come to visit me, you would be seen. Our present agencies would hear about it, and they might be alarmed. I don't want to alarm them."

If I were a client, I would do everything in my power to emancipate my agencies from fear, even to the extent of giving them long-term contracts.

My friend Clarence Eldridge has worked on both sides of the fence. After distinguishing himself as Chairman of the Plans Board at Young & Rubicam, he went on to become Vice President in charge of marketing for General Foods and later Senior Vice President of Campbell Soup Company. This judicious connoisseur of client-agency relationships came to believe that "there is one word which characterizes the ideal relationship: PERMANENCY . . . If permanency is to be achieved, it must be in the minds of the parties from the very beginning. It must be deliberately and consciously built into the relationship."

Arthur Page employed N. W. Ayer as the agency for American Telephone & Telegraph. Every now and then he would become disenchanted with Ayer's service, but instead of firing the agency, as most clients would have done, he summoned the head of Ayer and asked him to put things right. As a result, the AT&T advertising was never jolted by those dislocations which always accompany the appointment of a new agency. One Ayer man, George Cecil, wrote the AT&T copy for thirty years, and succeeded in building an image so favorable that it made a monopoly popular in a country which has no love for monopolies. Arthur Page was a wise client.

Advertising agencies make convenient scapegoats. It is easier to fire your agency than to admit to your stockholders that there is something wrong with your product or your management. However, before you fire your agency, ask yourself these questions:

(A) Procter & Gamble and General Foods get superlative service out of their agencies, and they have never fired an agency. Why not?

(B) Will the appointment of a new agency solve your problem, or merely sweep it under the rug? What are the real *roots* of your problem?

(C) Has your product been made obsolete by your competitors?

(D) Did you dictate the advertising for which you now blame your agency?

(E) Have you been scaring your agency into a blue funk?

(F) Is your advertising manager such a jackass that he would negate the best brains in *any* agency?

(G) How do you feel about one of your competitors inheriting the secrets which your agency has acquired in your service?

(H) Do you realize that a change in agencies may disrupt your marketing operation for twelve months or more?

(I) Have you been candid with the head of your agency? If you told him of your dissatisfaction, he might well be able to wheel up guns with greater fire power than you could find in a new agency.

(J) Have you faced the fact that when you dismiss an agency, you cause most of the men and women who work on your account to lose their jobs? Is there no way to avoid this human tragedy?

Several times I have advised manufacturers who wanted to hire our agency to stay where they were. For example, when the head of Hallmark Cards sent emissaries to sound me out, I said to them, "Your agency has contributed much to your fortunes. It would be an act of gross ingratitude to appoint another agency. Tell them exactly what it is about their service which you now find unsatisfactory. I am sure they will put it right. Stay where you are." Hallmark took my advice.

When one of the can companies invited us to solicit their account, I said, "Your agency has been giving you superb service, in circumstances of notorious difficulty. I happen to know that they lose money on your account. Instead of firing them, reward them."

One of the young Can executives bridled. "Mr. Ogilvy, that is the most impudent thing I have ever heard anyone say." But his colleagues decided that I was right.

When the Glass Container Manufacturers Institute asked us to compete for their account, I urged them to stay with Kenyon & Eckhardt, who had been giving them excellent advertising. They ignored my advice.

(2) *Select the right agency in the first place.*

If you spend large sums of your stockholders' money on advertising, and if your profits are dependent on its efficiency, it is your duty to take great pains to find the best possible agency.

Amateurs do it by cajoling a group of agencies into submitting free campaigns, on speculation. The agencies which win these contests are the ones which use their best brains for soliciting new accounts; they relegate their clients to their second-best brains. If I were a manufacturer, I would look for an agency which had no new-business department. The best agencies don't need them; they get all the business they can handle without preparing speculative campaigns.

The sensible way to pick an agency is to employ an advertising manager who knows enough about what is going on in the advertising world to have an informed judgment. Ask him to show you representative advertisements and commercials from the three or four agencies he believes to be best qualified for your account.

Then call some of their clients on the telephone. This can be particularly revealing when you call advertisers like Procter & Gamble, Lever, Colgate, General Foods, and Bristol-Myers, who employ *several* agencies; they can give you cross-bearings on most of the top agencies.

Then invite the chief executive from each of the leading contenders to bring two of his key men to dine at your house. Loosen their tongues. Find out if they are discreet about the secrets of their present clients. Find out if they have the spine to disagree when you say something stupid. Observe their relationship with each other; are they professional colleagues or quarrelsome politicians? Do they promise you results which are obviously exaggerated? Do they sound like extinct volcanoes, or are they alive? Are they good listeners? Are they intellectually honest?

Above all, find out if you *like* them; the relationship between client and agency has to be an intimate one, and it can be hell if the personal chemistry is sour.

Don't make the mistake of assuming that your account will be neglected in a *big* agency. The young men at the working levels in big agencies are often abler and harder-working than the nabobs at the top. On the other hand, don't assume that a big agency can give you more service than a small one. The number of bodies deployed against your account will be roughly the same in a small agency as in a big one – about nine bodies for every million dollars you spend.

(3) *Brief your agency very thoroughly indeed.*

The more your agency knows about your company and your

product, the better job it will do for you. When General Foods hired our agency to advertise Maxwell House Coffee, they undertook to teach us the coffee business. Day after day we sat at the feet of their experts, being lectured about green coffee, and blending, and roasting, and pricing, and the arcane economics of the industry.

Some advertising managers are too lazy or too ignorant to brief their agencies properly. In such cases we have to dig out the facts by ourselves. The resulting delay in producing our first campaign demoralizes all concerned.

(4) *Do not compete with your agency in the creative area.*

Why keep a dog and bark yourself?

Back-seat driving knocks the stuffing out of good creative men; if you do that, God help you. Make it plain to your advertising manager that the responsibility for creating your campaign belongs not to him but to the agency, and enjoin him not to dilute their responsibility.

When Ellerton Jetté offered us the Hathaway account he said: "We are about to start advertising. Our account will be less than $30,000 a year. If you will take it on, I will make you a promise: I will never change a word of your copy."

So we took the Hathaway account, and Mr. Jetté kept his word. He never changed a word of our copy. He saddled us with the *total* responsibility for his advertising. If our advertising for Hathaway had failed, the responsibility would have been mine. But it has *not* failed. Never has a national brand been built at such a low cost.

(5) *Coddle the goose who lays your golden eggs.*

Perhaps the most important operation agencies are ever called upon to perform is to prepare a campaign for a new product which has not yet emerged from the laboratory. This requires us to create a total image *ab ovo*.

As I write I am engaged in just such an operation. It has taken more than a hundred scientists two years to find out how to make the product in question; I have been given thirty days to create its personality and plan its launching. If I do my job well, I shall contribute as much as the hundred scientists to the success of this product.

This is not work for beginners. It calls for vivid imagination, tempered by marketing acumen; knowledge of the research techniques which should be used to select names, packages, and promises; an ability to peer into the future, when competitors will launch exactly similar products; and, not least, a genius for writing introductory advertisements. I doubt whether there are more than a dozen people in the United States who are qualified by temperament and experience to perform such an operation; and most clients expect it to be performed at the agency's expense. If they would invest half as much in the creative work of launching new products as they invest in the technical work of developing them, they would see fewer of their conceptions abort.

(6) *Don't strain your advertising through too many levels.*

I know one advertiser who makes his agencies clear their campaigns through five different levels in his company, each level having the power to tamper and veto.

This has grave consequences. It can cause leakage of secret information. It ties up able men in an interminable series of unnecessary meetings. It complicates the pristine simplicity of the original submissions. And, worst of all, it poisons the atmosphere with "creative politics." The copywriters learn to collect votes by pandering to the whims of a dozen different executives. When a copywriter becomes a politician, he qualifies for John Webster's description: "A politician imitates the Devil, as the Devil imitates a cannon: wheresoever he comes to do mischief, he comes with his backside towards you." (*The White Devil*, c. 1608).

Much of the messy advertising you see on television today is the product of committees. Committees can criticize advertisements, but they should never be allowed to create them.

Most of the campaigns which have built brands to fame and fortune have come from the partnership of two men – a sure-footed copywriter working in harness with an inspiring client. Such was the partnership of Gordon Seagrove and Jerry Lambert in building Listerine. And such was the partnership of Ted Moscoso and myself in advertising Puerto Rico.

When the Seagram people commissioned us to do a campaign for the Christian Brothers wines, they warned me that the advertisements would have to please not only their chieftain, Sam Bronfman, but also Brother Cellarmaster and his fellow monks at the Christian Brothers monastery in the Napa Valley. As a schoolboy I had loved Daudet's yarn about Père Gauchet, the monk who became an alcoholic while experimenting in search of the perfect liqueur. I therefore decided to make Brother Cellarmaster the hero of our campaign.

Seagram approved, and Brother Cellarmaster himself did not flinch from assuming the role of an ecclesiastical Commander Whitehead. But he felt obliged to submit our layouts to the head of his order in Rome, and that eminent divine turned thumbs down, in Latin. Shortly afterward one of the American cardinals intervened, and I was commanded to prepare a campaign "without impact." This unusual order took the wind out of my sails, and in due course I handed in my *nunc dimittis.* Hydra-headed clients present insoluble problems.

(7) *Make sure that your agency makes a profit.*

Your account competes with all the other accounts in your agency. If it is unprofitable, it is unlikely that the management of the agency will assign their best men to work on it. And sooner or later they will cast about for a profitable account to replace yours.

It has become increasingly difficult for agencies to make any profit at all. On every one hundred dollars spent by agencies on behalf of their clients, they now make an average profit of thirty-four cents. At this rate, the game is hardly worth the candle.

Experience has taught me that advertisers get the best results when they pay their agency a flat fee. The conventional 15-per-cent commission system is an anachronism, particularly on "package" goods accounts, where the agency is expected to give objective advice on the division of marketing expenditures between commissionable advertising and uncommissionable promotions. It is unrealistic to expect your agency to be impartial when its vested interest lies wholly in the direction of increasing your commissionable advertising.

It seems to me that the client-agency relationship is most satisfactory when the agency's emoluments are not related to the amount of money it can persuade its clients to spend on advertising. I prefer to be in a position to advise my clients to spend more without their suspecting my motive. And I like to be in a position to advise clients to spend *less* – without incurring the odium of my own stockholders.

I am not afraid of a price war between agencies. A period of competitive pricing would strengthen the good agencies and put the poor ones out of business. The whole standard of agency performance would be raised. Good agencies should be paid at a higher rate than bad ones.

My announcement that Ogilvy, Benson & Mather was prepared to handle accounts on a fee basis was greeted with approval by many thoughtful men outside the agency business. The head of McKinsey & Company wrote, "Your announcement shows real leadership in attacking publicly an outmoded method of compensation." Clarence Eldridge wrote, "You are to be congratulated on the courage to break with tradition and approach the matter of agency compensation logically and realistically. This represents a major breakthrough."

But my conversion to the fee system was so unpopular with my fellow advertising agents that it almost brought about our excommunication from the American Association of Advertising Agencies, on whose board I was then sitting.

For thirty years this august society had contrived to fix the price of agency service at 15 per cent, and membership of the Association had been contingent upon unswerving obedience to the rule. In

1956 the United States Government intervened to forbid its enforcement, but the tradition remained. Any advertising agent who rejected the conventional commission arrangement was a cad.

I prophesy that Madison Avenue opinion will change. Indeed, I expect to be remembered as the heretic who pioneered a course which conferred professional status on advertising agents.

(8) *Don't haggle with your agency.*

If you allow pettifoggers on your staff to haggle with your agency over payment of its bills, you make a mistake.

If, for example, you are stingy about paying for research, you will wind up without *enough* research. Your agency will be forced to fly blind. This could cost you your company.

If, on the other hand, you volunteer to pay for pretesting commercials, split-running experimental print advertisements, and all the other apparatus of advertising research, you will make it financially possible for your agency to experiment in continuous search for more profitable advertising.

Don't expect your agency to pay for all the dry holes they drill on your behalf. If, for example, they produce a television commercial which doesn't work as well as the storyboard promised, ask them to try again, *at your expense.* Television is an infernally difficult medium to use. I have not yet seen a commercial which satisfied me, but I cannot afford to pay $10,000 of my own money to remake one.

When we finished producing our first commercial for Vim detergent tablets, a wise man at Lever Brothers said to me, "Can you think of any ways in which this commercial could be improved?"

I confessed that I could think of nineteen ways. "Well," he said, "we are going to spend $4,000,000 on broadcasting this commercial. I want it to be as powerful as possible. Remake it, and we will pay for it." Most clients would have insisted that the agency pay for remaking it, an attitude that encourages agencies to conceal their divine discontent with their botches.

When Arthur Houghton asked us to do the advertising for Steuben, he gave me a crystal-clear directive: "We make the best glass in the world. Your job is to make the best advertising."

I replied, "Making perfect glass is very difficult. Even the Steuben craftsmen produce some imperfect pieces. Your inspectors break them. Making perfect advertisements is equally difficult."

Six weeks later I showed him the proof of our first Steuben advertisement. It was in color, and the plates, which had cost $1,200, were imperfect. Without demur, Arthur agreed to let me break them and make a new set. For such enlightened clients it is impossible to do shoddy work.

(9) *Be candid, and encourage candor.*

If you think that your agency is performing badly, or if you think that a particular advertisement is feeble, don't beat about the bush. Speak your mind, loud and clear. Disastrous consequences can arise when a client pussyfoots in his day-to-day dealings with his agency.

I do not suggest that you should threaten. Don't say, "You are an incompetent mucker, and I will get another agency unless you come back tomorrow with a great advertisement." Such brutality will only paralyze the troops. It is better to say, "What you have just shown me is not up to your usual high standard. Please take another crack at it." At the same time you should explain exactly what you find inadequate about the submission; don't leave your agency to guess.

This kind of candor will encourage your agency to be equally candid with you. And no partnership can fructify without candor on both sides.

(10) *Set high standards.*

Discourage bunting. Make it plain that you expect your agency to hit home runs, and pour on the praise when they do.

Many clients find it easy to blame their agency when sales go down, but are niggardly in giving credit to their agency when sales go up. This is unedifying.

But never let your agency rest on its laurels. Keep urging them to greater heights. You may have a good campaign going for you. The day after you first approve it, ask your agency to start searching for an *even better* one.

As soon as you find a campaign which tests better than the campaign you are now running, switch to it. But never give up a campaign just because you have grown tired of it; housewives don't see your advertisements as often as you do.

The best thing is to get a great campaign, and then continue it for several years. The problem is to *find* a great campaign. They don't grow on every tree, as you would know if you had my job of producing them.

(11) *Test everything.*

The most important word in the vocabulary of advertising is TEST. If you pretest your product with consumers, and pretest your advertising, you will do well in the marketplace.

Twenty-four out of twenty-five new products never get out of test markets. Manufacturers who *don't* test-market their products incur the colossal cost (and disgrace) of having their products fail on a national scale, instead of dying inconspicuously and economically in test markets.

Test your promise. Test your media. Test your headlines and your illustrations. Test the size of your advertisements. Test your frequency. Test your level of expenditure. Test your commercials. Never stop testing, and your advertising will never stop improving.

(12) *Hurry.*

Most young men in big corporations behave as if profit were not a function of time. When Jerry Lambert scored his first break-through with Listerine, he speeded up the whole process of marketing by dividing time into *months*. Instead of locking himself into *annual* plans, Lambert reviewed his advertising and his profits every month. The result was that he made $25,000,000 in eight years, where it takes most people twelve times as long. In Jerry Lambert's day, the Lambert Pharmacal Company lived by the month, instead of by the year. I commend that course to all advertisers.

(13) *Don't waste time on problem babies.*

Most advertisers and their agencies spend too much time worrying about how to revive products which are in trouble, and too little time worrying about how to make successful products even more successful. In advertising, it is the mark of a brave man to look unfavorable test results in the face, cut your loss, and move on.

You need not always drop the product. Sometimes you can make large profits out of "milking." Very few marketers know *how* to milk dying brands. It is like playing a misère hand in whist.

Concentrate your time, your brains, and your advertising money on your *successes*. Recognize success when it comes, and pour on the advertising. Back your winners, and abandon your losers.

(14) *Tolerate genius.*

Conan Doyle wrote that "mediocrity knows nothing higher than itself." My observation has been that mediocre men recognize genius, resent it, and feel compelled to destroy it.

There are very few men of genius in advertising agencies. But we need all we can find. Almost without exception they are disagreeable. Don't destroy them. They lay golden eggs.

(15) *Don't underspend.*

Says Charlie Mortimer, the head of General Foods and that

company's former advertising manager, "The surest way to over-spend on advertising is not to spend enough to do a job properly. It's like buying a ticket three-quarters of the way to Europe; you have spent some money, but you do not arrive."

I have come to think that nine out of ten advertising budgets are too small to do the job assigned to them. If your brand generates less than $2,000,000 a year for advertising, do not attempt contin-uous national advertising. Pull in your horns. Concentrate what money you have in your most lucrative markets, or confine your advertising to one income group. Or give up advertising completely. I hate to admit it, but there are other roads to fortune.

V How to Build Great Campaigns

When copywriters, art directors, and television producers come to work in our agency, they are herded into a conference room and subjected to my Magic Lantern, which tells them how to write headlines and body copy, how to illustrate advertisements, how to construct television commercials, and how to select the basic promise for their campaigns. The rules I postulate do not represent my personal opinions; they are the quintessence of what I have learned from research.

The recruits react to my lecture in different ways. Some find comfort and security under the command of a chief who seems to know what he is talking about. Some are uneasy at the prospect of working within such rigid disciplines.

"Surely," they say, "these rules and regulations must result in dull advertising?"

"*Not so far,*" I reply. And I go on to preach the importance of discipline in art. Shakespeare wrote his sonnets within a strict discipline, fourteen lines of iambic pentameter, rhyming in three quatrains and a couplet. Were his sonnets dull? Mozart wrote his sonatas within an equally rigid discipline – exposition, development, and recapitulation. Were *they* dull?

This argument disarms most of the highbrows. I go on to promise them that if they will subscribe to my principles, they will soon be producing good advertisements.

What is a good advertisement? There are three schools of thought. The cynics hold that a good advertisement is an advertisement with a client's OK on it. Another school accepts Raymond Rubicam's definition, "The best identification of a great advertisement is that its public is not only strongly sold by it, but that both the public and the advertising world remember it for a long time as an *admirable piece of work* . . ." I have produced my share of advertisements which have been remembered by the advertising world as "admirable pieces of work," but I belong to the third school, which holds that a good advertisement is one which sells the product *without drawing attention to itself*. It should rivet the reader's attention on the product. Instead of saying, "What a clever advertisement," the reader says, "I never knew *that* before. I must try this product."

It is the professional duty of the advertising agent to conceal his artifice. When Aeschines spoke, they said, "How well he speaks." But when Demosthenes spoke, they said, "Let us march against Philip." I'm for Demosthenes.

If my new recruits boggle at this stern definition of good advertising, I invite them to return to their previous incarnations, there to flounder in silliness and ignorance.

My next step is to tell them that I will not allow them to use the word CREATIVE to describe the functions they are to perform in our agency. The even more fashionable word CREATIVITY is not in the twelve-volume Oxford Dictionary. It reminds Leo Burnett of a saying of Bernard Berenson to the effect that the only thing the Etruscans added to the art of the Greeks was "the originality of incompetence." Fairfax Cone "would like to blot the word CREATIVITY out of our lives." Ed Cox thinks that "there are no creative or non-creative copywriters; only good ad-makers and bad." Bear in mind that Burnett, Cone, and Cox are among the most "creative" men in the advertising business. How did we get along twenty years ago, before "creativity" entered the lexicon of advertising? I am ashamed to say that I sometimes use it myself, even as I write these pages.

In this chapter I will expose to the reader what he would see in my Magic Lantern on the day he came to work for Ogilvy, Benson & Mather. The research on which it is based derives from five principal sources:

First, from the experience of mail-order advertisers. This elité corps, represented by such masters as Harry Scherman of the Book-of-the-Month Club, Vic Schwab, and John Caples, knows more about the *realities* of advertising than anybody else. They are in a position to measure the results of every advertisement they write, because their view is not obscured by those complex channels of distribution which make it impossible for most manufacturers to dissect out the results of their advertising from all the other factors in their marketing mix.

The mail-order advertiser has no retailers to shrink and expand their inventories, to push his product or to hide it under the counter. He must rely on his advertisements to do the entire selling job. Either the reader clips the coupon, or he doesn't. A few days after his advertisement appears, the mail-order writer knows whether it is profitable or not.

For twenty-seven years I have kept my eyes riveted on what mail-order advertisers do in their advertisements. And from this observation I have crystallized some general principles which can be applied, I believe, to all kinds of advertising.

The *second* most valuable source of information as to what makes some techniques succeed and others fail is the experience of department stores. The day after they run an advertisement, they can count the sales it has produced. That is why I am so attentive to the advertising practices of Sears, Roebuck, who are the most knowing of all retailers.

The *third* source of data on which my Magic Lantern depends is the research done by Gallup, Starch, Clark-Hooper and Harold Rudolph on the factors which make people *read* advertisements and, in the case of Dr. Gallup, the factors which make people *remember* what they read. On the whole, their findings endorse the experience of the mail-order fraternity.

More is known about consumer reactions to advertising in news-papers and magazines than consumer reactions to television commercials, because serious research into television – my *fourth* source – was not started until ten years ago. However, Dr. Gallup and others have already produced a body of knowledge about tele-vision advertising which is sufficient to emancipate us from *total* reliance on guesswork. (When it comes to *radio* commercials, there is little or no research available from any source. Radio was made obsolete by television before anybody had learned to use it scientifically, but it has now recovered to the point where it may be described as the Cinderella of advertising media; it is time for the researchers to tackle it.)

My last source is less scientific. I am an inveterate brainpicker, and the most rewarding brains I have picked are the brains of my pred-ecessors and my competitors. I have learned much from studying the successful campaigns of Raymond Rubicam, Jim Young, and George Cecil.

Here, then, are my recipes for cooking up the kind of advertising campaigns which make the cash register ring – eleven commandments which you must obey if you work at my agency:

(1) *What You Say Is More Important Than How You Say It.*

Once upon a time I was riding on the top of a Fifth Avenue bus, when I heard a mythical housewife say to another, "Molly, my dear, I would have bought that new brand of toilet soap if only they hadn't set the body copy in ten point Garamond."

Don't you believe it. What really decides consumers to buy or not to buy is the *content* of your advertising, not its form. Your most important job is to decide what you are going to say about your product, what benefit you are going to promise. Two hundred years ago Dr. Johnson said, "Promise, large promise is the soul of an advertisement." When he auctioned off the contents of the Anchor Brewery he made the following promise: "We are not here to sell boilers and vats, but the potentiality of growing rich beyond the dreams of avarice."

The selection of the right promise is so vitally important that you should never rely on *guesswork* to decide it. At Ogilvy, Benson & Mather, we use five research techniques to find out which is the most powerful.

One technique is to distribute batches of the product to matched samples of consumers, each batch bearing a different promise on the package. Then we compare the percentages of consumers in each sample who send us a repeat order.

Another technique is to show consumers cards on which we have printed various promises, asking them to select the one which would be most likely to make them buy the product. Here are the results of one such test:

FACE CREAM

Cleans Deep into Pores ▬▬▬▬▬▬▬▬▬▬▬▬
Prevents Dryness ▬▬▬▬▬▬▬▬▬▬▬▬▬
Is a Complete Beauty Treatment ▬▬▬▬▬▬▬▬
Recommended by Skin Doctors ▬▬▬▬▬▬▬▬
Makes Skin Look Younger ▬▬▬▬▬▬▬
Prevents Make-up Caking ▬▬▬▬▬
Contains Estrogenic Hormones ▬▬▬
Pasteurized for Purity ▬▬▬
Prevents Skin from Aging ▬
Smooths Out Wrinkles ▬

From this voting came one of Helena Rubinstein's most successful face creams. We christened it Deep Cleanser, thus building the winning promise into the name of the product.

Another technique is to prepare a series of advertisements, each built around a different promise. We then mail the advertisements to matched samples and count the number of orders procured by each promise.

Another technique is to run pairs of advertisements in the same position in the same issue of a newspaper, with an offer of a sample buried in the copy. We used this artful dodge to select the strongest promise for Dove toilet bar. "Creams Your Skin While You Wash" pulled 63 per cent more orders than the next best promise, and it has been the fulcrum of every Dove advertisement that has ever run. This marvelous product made a profit at the end of its first year, a rare feat in the marketing world of today.

Finally, we have developed a technique for selecting basic promises which is so valuable that my partners forbid me to reveal it. They remind me of that selfish family of eighteenth-century obstetricians who made a fortune by delivering more live babies than any of their competitors. They kept their secret for three generations; it was not until an enterprising medical student climbed up and peeked through the window of their surgery that the design of their forceps was revealed to the world.

(2) *Unless Your Campaign Is Built Around a Great Idea, it Will Flop.*

It isn't every client who can recognize a great idea when he sees it. I remember presenting a truly brilliant idea to a client who said, "Mr. Ogilvy, you have here the *mucus* of a good idea."

When I started writing advertisements, I was determined to blaze new trails, to make every one of my campaigns the most successful in the history of the industry concerned. I have not always failed.

(3) *Give the Facts.*

Very few advertisements contain enough factual information to sell the product. There is a ludicrous tradition among copywriters that consumers aren't interested in facts. Nothing could be farther from the truth. Study the copy in the Sears, Roebuck catalogue; it sells a billion dollars' worth of merchandise every year by giving *facts*. In my Rolls-Royce advertisements I gave nothing but facts. No adjectives, no "gracious living."

The consumer isn't a moron; she is your wife. You insult her intelligence if you assume that a mere slogan and a few vapid adjectives will persuade her to buy anything. She wants all the information you can give her.

Competing brands are becoming more and more alike. The men who make them have access to the same scientific journals; they use the same production techniques; and they are guided by the same research. When faced with the inconvenient fact that their brand is about the same as several others, most copywriters conclude that there is no point in telling the consumer what is common to all brands; so they confine themselves to some trivial point of difference. I hope that they will continue to make this mistake, because it enables us to *pre-empt the truth* for our clients.

When we advertise Shell, we give the consumer *facts*, many of which other gasoline marketers could give, but don't. When we advertise KLM Royal Dutch Airlines we tell travelers about the safety precautions which all airlines take, but fail to mention in their advertisements.

When I was a door-to-door salesman I discovered that the more information I gave about my product, the more I sold. Claude Hopkins made the same discovery about advertising, fifty years ago. But most modern copywriters find it easier to write short, lazy advertisements. Collecting facts is hard work.

(4) *You Cannot Bore People into Buying.*

The average family is now exposed to more than 1500 advertisements a day. No wonder they have acquired a talent for skipping the advertisements in newspapers and magazines, and going to the bathroom during television commercials.

The average woman now reads only four of the advertisements which appear in the average magazine. She *glances* at more, but one glance is enough to tell her that the advertisement is too boring to read.

Competition for the consumer's attention is becoming more ferocious every year. She is being bombarded by a billion dollars' worth of advertising a month. Thirty thousand brand names are competing for a place in her memory. If you want your voice to be heard above this ear-splitting barrage, your voice must be unique. It is our business to make our clients' voices heard above the crowd.

We make advertisements that people want to read. You can't save souls in an empty church. If you will embrace our rules, you will be able to reach more readers per dollar.

I once asked Sir Hugh Rigby, Sergeant Surgeon to King George V, "What makes a great surgeon?"

Sir Hugh replied, "There isn't much to choose between surgeons in manual dexterity. What distinguishes the great surgeon is that he *knows* more than other surgeons." It is the same with advertising agents. The good ones know their craft.

(5) *Be Well-Mannered, But Don't Clown.*

People don't buy from bad-mannered salesmen, and research has shown that they don't buy from bad-mannered advertisements. It is easier to sell people with a friendly handshake than by hitting them over the head with a hammer. You should try to *charm* the consumer into buying your product.

This doesn't mean that your advertisements should be cute or comic. People don't buy from clowns. When the housewife fills her shopping basket, she is in a fairly serious frame of mind.

(6) *Make Your Advertising Contemporary.*

The young housewife of 1963 was born after President Roosevelt died. She is living in a new world. At the age of fifty-one I am finding it increasingly difficult to tune in on the young married couples who are starting out in life; that is why most of the copywriters at our agency are so young. They understand the psychology of young consumers better than I do.

(7) *Committees Can Criticize Advertisements, But They Cannot Write Them.*

A lot of advertisements and television commercials look like the minutes of a committee meeting, and that is what they are. Advertising seems to sell most when it is written by a solitary individual. He must study the product, the research, and the precedents. Then he must shut the door of his office and write the advertisement. The best advertisement I ever wrote went through seventeen drafts, and built a business.

(8) *If You Are Lucky Enough To Write a Good Advertisement, Repeat It Until It Stops Pulling.*

Scores of good advertisements have been discarded before they lost their potency, largely because their sponsors got sick of seeing them. Sterling Getchel's famous advertisement for Plymouth ("Look at All Three") appeared only once, and was succeeded by a series of inferior variations which were quickly forgotten. But the Sherwin Cody School of English ran the same advertisement ("Do You Make These Mistakes in English?") for forty-two years, changing only the type face and the color of Mr. Cody's beard.

You aren't advertising to a standing army; you are advertising to a moving parade. Three million consumers get married every year. The advertisement which sold a refrigerator to those who got married last year will probably be just as successful with those who get married next year. One million, seven hundred thousand consumers die every year, and 4,000,000 new ones are born. They enter the market and they depart from it. An advertisement is like a radar sweep, constantly hunting new prospects as they come into the market. *Get a good radar, and keep it sweeping.*

(9) *Never Write an Advertisement Which You Wouldn't Want Your Own Family To Read.*

You wouldn't tell lies to your own wife. Don't tell them to mine. Do as you would be done by.

If you tell lies about a product, you will be found out – either by the Government, which will prosecute you, or by the consumer, who will punish you by not buying your product a second time.

Good products can be sold by *honest* advertising. If you don't think the product is good, you have no business to be advertising it. If you tell lies, or weasel, you do your client a disservice, you increase your load of guilt, and you fan the flames of public resentment against the whole business of advertising.

(10) *The Image and the Brand.*

Every advertisement should be thought of as a contribution to the complex symbol which is the *brand image.* If you take that long view, a great many day-to-day problems solve themselves.

How do you decide what kind of image to build? There is no short answer. Research cannot help you much here. You have actually got to use judgment. (I notice increasing reluctance on the part of marketing executives to use judgment; they are coming to rely too much on research, and they use it as a drunkard uses a lamp post, for support rather than for illumination.)

Most manufacturers are reluctant to accept any *limitation* on the image of their brand. They want it to be all things to all people. They want their brand to be a male brand *and* a female brand. An upper-crust brand *and* a plebeian brand. They generally end up with a brand which has no personality of any kind, a wishy-washy neuter. No capon ever rules the roost.

Ninety-five per cent of all the campaigns now in circulation are being created without any reference to such long-term considerations. They are being created *ad hoc.* Hence the lack of any consistent image from one year to another.

What a miracle it is when a manufacturer manages to sustain a coherent style in his advertising over a period of years! Think of all the forces that work to change it. The advertising managers come and go. The copywriters come and go. Even the agencies come and go.

It takes uncommon guts to stick to one style in the face of all the pressures to "come up with something new" every six months. It is tragically easy to be stampeded into change.

But golden rewards await the advertiser who has the brains to create a coherent image, and the stability to stick with it over a long period. As examples, I cite Campbell Soup, Ivory Soap, Esso, Betty Crocker, and Guinness Stout (in England). The men who have been responsible for the advertising of these hardy perennials have understood that every advertisement, every radio program, every TV commercial is not a one-time shot, but a long-term investment in the total personality of their brands. They have presented a consistent image to the world, and grown rich in the process.

During the last few years the researchers have been able to tell us what image old brands have acquired in the public mind. Some manufacturers have been sobered to learn that their image has serious flaws, which have been hurting their sales. They then ask their advertising agency to set about *changing* the image. This is one of the most difficult operations we are ever called upon to perform, because the faulty image has been built up over a period of many years. It is the result of many different factors – advertising, pricing, the name of the product, its packaging, the kind of television shows it has sponsored, the length of time it has been on the market, and so on.

Most of the manufacturers who find it expedient to change the image of their brand want it changed *upward*. Often it has acquired a bargain-basement image, a useful asset in times of economic scarcity, but a grave embarrassment in boom days, when the majority of consumers are on their way up the social ladder.

It isn't easy to perform a face-lifting operation on an old bargain-basement brand. In many cases it would be easier to start again, with a fresh new brand.

The greater the similarity between brands, the less part reason plays in brand selection. There isn't any significant difference between the various brands of whiskey, or cigarettes, or beer. They are all about the same. And so are the cake mixes and the detergents, and the margarines.

The manufacturer who dedicates his advertising to building the most sharply defined *personality* for his brand will get the largest share of the market at the highest profit. By the same token, the manufacturers who will find themselves up the creek are those shortsighted opportunists who siphon off their advertising funds for promotions. Year after year I find myself warning my clients about what will happen to their brands if they spend so much on promotions that there is no money left for advertising.

Price-off deals and other such hypodermics find favor with sales managers, but their effect is ephemeral, and they can be habit-forming. Says Bev Murphy, who invented Art Nielsen's technique for measuring consumer purchases and went on to become President of Campbell Soup Company: "Sales are a function of product-value and advertising. *Promotions cannot produce more than a temporary kink in the sales curve.*" Jerry Lambert never used promotions for Listerine; he knew that kinks in a sales curve make it impossible to read out the results of advertising.

A steady diet of price-off promotions lowers the esteem in which the consumer holds the product; can anything which is always sold at a discount be desirable?

Plan your campaign for years ahead, on the assumption that your clients intend to stay in business forever. Build sharply defined personalities for their brands, and stick to those personalities, year after year. It is the total personality of a brand rather than any trivial product difference which decides its ultimate position in the market.

(11) *Don't Be a Copy-Cat.*

Rudyard Kipling wrote a long poem about a self-made shipping tycoon called Sir Anthony Gloster. On his death bed the old man reviews the course of his life for the benefit of his son, and refers contemptuously to his competitors:

> They copied all they could follow, but they
> couldn't copy my mind,
> And I left 'em sweating and stealing, a year
> and a half behind.

If you ever have the good fortune to create a great advertising campaign, you will soon see another agency steal it. This is irritating, but don't let it worry you; nobody has ever built a brand by imitating somebody else's advertising.

Imitation may be the "sincerest form of plagiarism," but it is also the mark of an inferior person.

These, then, are the general principles I inculcate in our new recruits. When I recently invited a group of them who had completed their first year with us to compare Ogilvy, Benson & Mather with their previous agencies, I was agreeably surprised by the number who fastened on the fact that we have a more clearly defined dogma. Here is what one of them wrote:

Ogilvy, Benson & Mather has a consistent point of view, a corporate opinion of what constitutes good advertising. My previous agency has none, and consequently is rudderless.

VI How to Write Potent Copy

I. Headlines

The headline is the most important element in most advertisements. It is the telegram which decides the reader whether to read the copy.

On the average, five times as many people read the headline as read the body copy. When you have written your headline, you have spent eighty cents out of your dollar.

If you haven't done some selling in your headline, you have wasted 80 per cent of your client's money. The wickedest of all sins is to run an advertisement *without* a headline. Such headless wonders are still to be found; I don't envy the copywriter who submits one to me.

A change of headline can make a difference of ten to one in sales. I never write fewer than sixteen headlines for a single advertisement, and I observe certain guides in writing them:

(1) The headline is the "ticket on the meat." Use it to flag down the readers who are prospects for the kind of product you are advertising. If you are selling a remedy for bladder weakness, display the words BLADDER WEAKNESS in your headline; they catch the eye of everyone who suffers from this inconvenience. If you want *mothers* to read your advertisement, display MOTHERS in your headline. And so on.

Conversely, do not say anything in your headline which is likely to *exclude* any readers who might be prospects for your product. Thus, if you are advertising a product which can be used equally well by men and women, don't slant your headline at women alone; it would frighten men away.

(2) Every headline should appeal to the reader's *self-interest* . . . It should promise her a benefit, as in my headline for Helena Rubinstein's Hormone Cream: HOW WOMEN OVER 35 CAN LOOK YOUNGER.

3) Always try to inject *news* into your headlines, because the consumer is always on the lookout for new products, or new ways to use an old product, or new improvements in an old product.

The two most powerful words you can use in a headline are FREE and NEW. You can seldom use FREE, but you can almost always use NEW – if you try hard enough.

(4) Other words and phrases which work wonders are:

HOW TO, SUDDENLY, NOW, ANNOUNCING, INTRODUCING, IT'S HERE, JUST ARRIVED, IMPORTANT DEVELOPMENT, IMPROVEMENT, AMAZING, SENSATIONAL, REMARKABLE, REVOLUTIONARY, STARTLING, MIRACLE, MAGIC, OFFER, QUICK, EASY, WANTED, CHALLENGE, ADVICE TO, THE TRUTH ABOUT, COMPARE, BARGAIN, HURRY, LAST CHANCE.

Don't turn up your nose at these clichés. They may be shopworn, but they work. That is why you see them turn up so often in the headlines of mail-order advertisers and others who can measure the results of their advertisements.

Headlines can be strengthened by the inclusion of *emotional* words, like DARLING, LOVE, FEAR, PROUD, FRIEND, and BABY. One of the most provocative advertisements which has come out of our agency showed a girl in a bathtub, talking to her lover on the telephone. The headline: *Darling, I'm having the most extraordinary experience . . . I'm head over heels in DOVE.*

(5) Five times as many people read the headline as read the body copy, so it is important that these glancers should at least be told what brand is being advertised. That is why you should always include the brand name in your headlines.

(6) Include your selling promise in your headline. This requires long headlines. When the New York University School of Retailing ran headline tests with the cooperation of a big department store, they found that headlines of ten words or longer, containing news and information, consistently sold more merchandise than short headlines.

Headlines containing six to twelve words pull more coupon returns than short headlines, and there is no significant difference between the readership of twelve-word headlines and the readership of three-word headlines. The best headline I ever wrote contained *eighteen* words: *At Sixty Miles an Hour the Loudest Noise in the New Rolls-Royce comes from the electric clock.**

(7) People are more likely to read your body copy if your headline arouses their curiosity; so you should end your headline with a lure to read on.

---

* When the chief engineer at the Rolls-Royce factory read this, he shook his head sadly and said, "It is time we did something about that damned clock."

(8) Some copywriters write *tricky* headlines – puns, literary allusions, and other obscurities. This is a sin.

In the average newspaper your headline has to compete for attention with 350 others. Research has shown that readers travel so fast through this jungle that they don't stop to decipher the meaning of obscure headlines. Your headline must *telegraph* what you want to say, and it must telegraph it in plain language. Don't play games with the reader.

In 1960 the *Times Literary Supplement* attacked the whimsical tradition in British advertising, calling it "self-indulgent – a kind of middle-class private joke, apparently designed to amuse the advertiser and his client." Amen.

(9) Research shows that it is dangerous to use *negatives* in headlines. If, for example, you write OUR SALT CONTAINS NO ARSENIC, many readers will miss the negative and go away with the impression that you wrote OUR SALT CONTAINS ARSENIC.

(10) Avoid *blind* headlines – the kind which mean nothing unless you read the body copy underneath them; most people *don't*.

II. Body Copy

When you sit down to write your body copy, pretend that you are talking to the woman on your right at a dinner party. She has asked you, "I am thinking of buying a new car. Which would you recommend?" Write your copy as if you were answering that question.

(1) Don't beat about the bush – go straight to the point. Avoid

analogies of the "just as, so too" variety. Dr. Gallup has demonstrated that these two-stage arguments are generally misunderstood.

(2) Avoid superlatives, generalizations, and platitudes. Be specific and factual. Be enthusiastic, friendly, and memorable. Don't be a bore. Tell the truth, but make the truth fascinating.

How long should your copy be? It depends on the product. If you are advertising chewing gum, there isn't much to tell, so make your copy short. If, on the other hand, you are advertising a product which has a great many different qualities to recommend it, write long copy: the more you tell, the more you sell.

There is a universal belief in lay circles that people won't read long copy. Nothing could be farther from the truth. Claude Hopkins once wrote five pages of solid text for Schlitz beer. In a few months, Schlitz moved up from fifth place to first. I once wrote a page of solid text for Good Luck Margarine, with most gratifying results.

Research shows that readership falls off rapidly up to fifty words of copy, but drops very little between fifty and 500 words. In my first Rolls-Royce advertisement I used 719 words – piling one fascinating fact on another. In the last paragraph I wrote, "People who feel diffident about driving a Rolls-Royce can buy a Bentley." Judging from the number of motorists who picked up the word "diffident" and bandied it about, I concluded that the advertisement was thoroughly read. In the next one I used 1400 words.

Every advertisement should be a *complete* sales pitch for your product. It is unrealistic to assume that consumers will read a *series* of advertisements for the same product. You should shoot the works in every advertisement, on the assumption that it is the only chance you will ever have to sell your product to the reader – *now or never*.

Says Dr. Charles Edwards of the graduate School of Retailing at New York University, "The more facts you tell, the more you sell. An advertisement's chance for success invariably increases as the number of pertinent merchandise facts included in the advertisement increases."

In my first advertisement for Puerto Rico's Operation Bootstrap, I used 961 words, and persuaded Beardsley Ruml to sign them. Fourteen thousand readers clipped the coupon from this advertisement, and scores of them later established factories in Puerto Rico. The greatest professional satisfaction I have yet had is to see the prosperity in Puerto Rican communities which had lived on the edge of starvation for four hundred years before I wrote my advertisement. If I had confined myself to a few vacuous generalities, nothing would have happened.

We have even been able to get people to read long copy about gasoline. One of our Shell advertisements contained 617 words, and 22 per cent of male readers read more than half of them.

Vic Schwab tells the story of Max Hart (of Hart, Schaffner & Marx) and his advertising manager, George L. Dyer, arguing about long copy. Dyer said, "I'll bet you ten dollars I can write a newspaper page of solid type and you'd read every word of it."

Hart scoffed at the idea. "I don't have to write a line of it to prove my point," Dyer replied. "I'll only tell you the headline: THIS PAGE IS ALL ABOUT MAX HART."

Advertisers who put coupons in their advertisements *know* that short copy doesn't sell. In split-run tests, long copy invariably outsells short copy.

Do I hear someone say that no copywriter can write long advertisements unless his media department gives him big spaces to work with? This question should not arise, because the copywriter should be consulted before planning the media schedule.

(3) You should always include testimonials in your copy. The reader finds it easier to believe the endorsement of a fellow consumer than the puffery of an anonymous copywriter. Says Jim Young, one of the best copywriters alive today, "Every type of advertiser has the same problem; namely to be believed. The mail-order man knows nothing so potent for this purpose as the testimonial, yet the general advertiser seldom uses it."

Testimonials from celebrities get remarkably high readership, and if they are honestly written they still do not seem to provoke incredulity. The better known the celebrity, the more readers you will attract. We have featured Queen Elizabeth and Winston Churchill in "Come to Britain" advertisements, and we were able to persuade Mrs. Roosevelt to make television commercials for Good Luck Margarine. When we advertised charge accounts for Sears, Roebuck, we reproduced the credit card of Ted Williams, "recently traded by Boston to Sears."

Sometimes you can cast your entire copy in the form of a testimonial. My first advertisement for Austin cars took the form of a letter from an "anonymous diplomat" who was sending his son to Groton with money he had saved driving an Austin – a well-aimed combination of snobbery and economy. Alas, a perspicacious *Time* editor guessed that I was the anonymous diplomat, and asked the headmaster of Groton to comment. Dr. Crocker was so cross that I decided to send my son to Hotchkiss.

(4) Another profitable gambit is to give the reader helpful advice, or service. It hooks about 75 per cent more readers than copy which deals entirely with the product.

One of our Rinso advertisements told housewives how to remove stains. It was better read (Starch) and better remembered (Gallup) than any detergent advertisement in history. Unfortunately, however, it forgot to feature Rinso's main selling promise – that Rinso washes whiter; for this reason it should never have run.*

(5) I have never admired the *belles lettres* school of advertising, which reached its pompous peak in Theodore F. MacManus' famous advertisement for Cadillac, "The Penalty of Leadership," and Ned Jordan's classic, "Somewhere West of Laramie." Forty years ago the business community seems to have been impressed by these pieces of purple prose, but I have always thought them absurd; they did not give the reader a single *fact* . . . I share Claude Hopkins' view that "fine writing is a distinct disadvantage. So is unique literary style. They take attention away from the subject."

(6) Avoid bombast. Raymond Rubicam's famous slogan for

---

* The photograph showed several different kinds of stain – lipstick, coffee, shoe-polish, blood and so forth. The blood was my own; I am the only copywriter who has ever *bled* for his client.

Squibb, "The priceless ingredient of every product is the honor and integrity of its maker," reminds me of my father's advice: when a company boasts about its integrity, or a woman about her virtue, avoid the former and cultivate the latter.

(7) Unless you have some special reason to be solemn and pretentious, write your copy in the colloquial language which your customers use in everyday conversation. I have never acquired a sufficiently good ear for vernacular American to write it, but I admire copywriters who can pull it off, as in this unpublished pearl from a dairy farmer:

> Carnation Milk is the best in the land,
> Here I sit with a can in my hand.
> No tits to pull, no hay to pitch,
> Just punch a hole in the son-of-a-bitch.

It is a mistake to use highfalutin language when you advertise to uneducated people. I once used the word OBSOLETE in a headline, only to discover that 43 per cent of housewives had no idea what it meant. In another headline, I used the word INEFFABLE, only to discover that I didn't know what it meant myself.

However, many copywriters of my vintage err on the side of underestimating the educational level of the population. Philip Hauser, head of the Sociology Department at the University of Chicago, draws attention to the changes which are taking place:

> The increasing exposure of the population to formal
> schooling . . . can be expected to effect important changes in
> . . . the style of advertising . . . . Messages aimed at the
> "average" American on the assumption that he has had less

than a grade school education are likely to find themselves
with a declining or disappearing clientele.*

Meanwhile, all copywriters should read Dr. Rudolph Flesch's *Art of
Plain Talk*. It will persuade them to use short words, short
sentences, short paragraphs, and highly *personal* copy.

Aldous Huxley, who once tried his hand at writing advertisements,
concluded that "any trace of literariness in an advertisement is
fatal to its success. Advertisement writers may not be lyrical, or
obscure, or in any way esoteric. They must be universally intelli-
gible. A good advertisement has this in common with drama and
oratory, that it must be immediately comprehensible and directly
moving." †

(8) Resist the temptation to write the kind of copy which wins
awards. I am always gratified when I win an award, but most of the
campaigns which produce *results* never win awards, because they
don't draw attention to themselves.

The juries that bestow awards are never given enough information
about the *results* of the advertisements they are called upon to
judge. In the absence of such information, they rely on their opinions, which are always warped toward the highbrow.

(9) Good copywriters have always resisted the temptation to *entertain*. Their achievement lies in the number of new products they
get off to a flying start. In a class by himself stands Claude Hopkins,

* *Scientific American* (October 1962),
† *Essays Old And New* (Harper & Brothers, 1927). Charles Lamb and Byron also
wrote advertisements. So did Bernard Shaw, Hemingway, Marquand, Sherwood
Anderson, and Faulkner – none of them with any degree of success.

who is to advertising what Escoffier is to cooking. By today's standards, Hopkins was an unscrupulous barbarian, but technically he was the supreme master. Next I would place Raymond Rubicam, George Cecil, and James Webb Young, all of whom lacked Hopkins' ruthless salesmanship, but made up for it by their honesty, by the broader range of their work, and by their ability to write civilized copy when the occasion required it. Next I would place John Caples, the mail-order specialist from whom I have learned much.

These giants wrote their advertisements for newspapers and magazines. It is still too early to identify the best writers for television.

VII How to Illustrate
Advertisements and Posters

Advertisements

MOST copywriters think in terms of words, and devote little time to planning their illustrations. Yet the illustration often occupies more space than the copy, and it should work just as hard to sell the product. It should telegraph the same promise that you make in your headline.

Doyle, Dane & Bernbach have a unique genius for illustrating advertisements; the photographs they have used for Volkswagen are in a class by themselves.

The *subject* of your illustration is more important than its *technique* . . . As in all areas of advertising, substance is more important than form. If you have a remarkable idea for a photograph, it does not require a genius to click the shutter. If you haven't got a remarkable idea, not even Irving Penn can save you.

Dr. Gallup has discovered that the kind of photographs which win awards from camera clubs – sensitive, subtle, and beautifully composed – don't work in advertisements. What do work are photographs which arouse the reader's *curiosity* . . . He glances at the photograph and says to himself, "What goes on here?" Then he reads your copy to find out. This is the trap to set.

Harold Rudolph called this magic element "story appeal," and demonstrated that the more of it you inject into your photographs, the more people will look at your advertisements. This discovery has had a profound effect on the campaigns produced by my agency.

When we were asked to preside over Hathaway's debut as a national advertiser, I was determined to give them a campaign which would be better than Young & Rubicam's historic campaign for Arrow shirts. But Hathaway could spend only $30,000 against Arrow's $2,000,000. A miracle was required.

Knowing from Rudolph that a strong dose of "story appeal" would make readers stop and take notice, I concocted eighteen different ways to inject this magic ingredient. The eighteenth was the eye patch. At first we rejected it in favor of a more obvious idea, but on the way to the studio I ducked into a drugstore and bought an eye patch for $1.50 . . . Exactly why it turned out to be so successful, I shall never know. It put Hathaway on the map after 116 years of relative obscurity. Seldom, if ever, has a national brand been created so fast, or at such low cost. Articles were written about it in newspapers and magazines all over the world. Scores of other manufacturers stole it for their own advertising – I have seen five copies from Denmark alone. What struck me as a moderately good idea for a wet Tuesday morning made me famous. I could have wished for fame to come from some more serious achievement.

As the campaign developed, I showed the model in a series of situations in which I would have liked to find myself: conducting the New York Philharmonic at Carnegie Hall, playing the oboe, copying a Goya at the Metropolitan Museum, driving a tractor, fencing, sailing, buying a Renoir, and so forth. After eight years of this, my friend Ellerton Jetté sold the Hathaway company to a

Boston financier, who resold it six months later at a profit of several million dollars. My total profit on the account had been $6,000 . . . If I were a financier instead of an advertising agent, how rich I would be, and how bored.

Another example of "story appeal" was a photograph which Elliott Erwitt took for our Puerto Rico tourism campaign. Instead of photographing Pablo Casals playing his cello, Erwitt photographed an empty room, with the great man's cello leaning against a chair. *Why was the room empty? Where was Casals?* Those were the questions raised in the reader's mind, and he looked for the answer in our copy. After reading it, he made reservations for the Casals Festival in San Juan. During the first six years of this campaign, tourist expenditures in Puerto Rico went up from $19,000,000 to $53,000,000 a year.

If you will take the trouble to get great photographs for your advertisements, you will not only sell more, you will also bask in the glow of public esteem. I was comforted when Professor J. K. Galbraith, that redoubtable critic of advertising, wrote to me, "For years I have been interested in photography, and for quite a long time I have picked out yours as really superb examples of both selection and reproduction."

Over and over again research has shown that *photographs* sell more than *drawings*. They attract more readers. They deliver more appetite appeal. They are better remembered. They pull more coupons. And they sell more merchandise. Photographs represent reality, whereas drawings represent fantasy, which is less believable.

When we took over the "Come to Britain" advertising we substituted photographs for the drawings which the previous agency had been using. Readership tripled, and in the subsequent ten years U.S. tourist expenditures in Britain have tripled.

It grieves me to tell you not to use drawings, because I would dearly like to help artists get commissions to illustrate advertisements. But the advertisements would not sell, the clients would go broke, and then there would be no patrons left to support the artists. If you use photographs, your clients will prosper sufficiently to buy paintings and present them to public galleries.

Some manufacturers illustrate their advertisements with abstract paintings. I would only do this if I wished to conceal from the reader what I was advertising. It is imperative that your illustration *telegraph* to the reader what it is that you are offering for sale. Abstract art does not telegraph its message fast enough for use in advertisements.

The only advertiser who ever made a success with nonrepresentational illustrations was the late Walter Paepcke. The eccentricity of his campaign for the Container Corporation seems to have set that company apart from its competitors; but it takes more than one swallow to make a summer. Reader, beware of eccentricity when you advertise to people who are not eccentric.

Before-and-after photographs seem to fascinate readers, and to make their point better than any words. So does a challenge to the reader to tell the difference between two similar photographs, as in "Which Twin Has the Toni?"

When in doubt as to which of two illustrations to use, test their relative pulling power by split-running them in a newspaper. We used this technique to settle a dispute over whether KLM advertisements should be illustrated with photographs of aircraft or photographs of destinations. The latter pulled twice as many coupons as the former. That is why all KLM advertisements are now illustrated with photographs of destinations.

When I worked for Dr. Gallup, I was able to demonstrate that moviegoers are more interested in actors of their own sex than in actors of the opposite sex. True, there are a few exceptions to this rule: the female sex-kittens find great favor with male moviegoers and the lesbian stars do not appeal to men. But, in general, people take more interest in movie stars with whom they can identify. In the same way, the cast of characters in most people's dreams contains more people of their own sex than of the opposite sex. Dr. Calvin Hall reports that "the male-female character ratio in male dreams is 1.7 to 1 . . . This . . . appears also in Hopi dreams . . . It may prove to be a universal phenomenon." *

I have observed the same force at work in consumer reactions to advertisements. When you use a photograph of a woman, men ignore your advertisement. When you use a photograph of a man, you exclude women from your audience.

If you want to attract women readers, your best bet is to use a photograph of a baby. Research has shown that they stop almost twice as many women as photographs of *families* . . . When you were a baby you were the cynosure of every eye, but by the time

* Dr. Hall's analysis of 3,874 dreams led him to some other remarkable conclusions, including these: "The faucet was invented by a man who wanted a better penis. Money was invented by someone who wanted to accumulate a bigger pile of feces. Rockets to the moon were invented by a group of dissatisfied oedipal animals. Houses were invented by wombseekers, and whiskey by breastlings."

you became a mere member of the family, you attracted no special attention.

Here you run into a peculiar difficulty. Most manufacturers object to illustrating babies in their advertisements, because babies consume such small tonnage; they want you to show the whole ruddy family.

One of the most agreeable chores in advertising is selecting pretty girls to appear in advertisements and television commercials. I used to arrogate this function to myself, but gave it up after comparing my personal taste in girls with the taste of female consumers. Men don't like the same kind of girls that girls like.

Advertisements are twice as memorable, on the average, when they are illustrated in *color*.

Avoid historical subjects. They may be useful for advertising whiskey, but for nothing else.

Don't show enlarged close-ups of the human face; they seem to repel readers.

Keep your illustrations as *simple* as possible, with the focus of interest on one person. Crowd scenes don't pull.

Avoid stereotyped situations like grinning housewives pointing fatuously into open refrigerators.

When you get into a jam, you may find this advice helpful:

> When the client moans and sighs,
> Make his logo twice the size.

> If he still should prove refractory,
> Show a picture of the factory.
> Only in the gravest cases
> Should you show the clients' faces.

"Making the logo twice the size" is often a good thing to do, because most advertisements are deficient in brand identification.

"Showing the clients' faces" is also a better stratagem than it may sound, because the public is more interested in personalities than in corporations. Some clients, like Helena Rubinstein and Commander Whitehead, can be projected as human symbols of their own products.

But it is never wise to "show a picture of the factory" – unless the factory is for sale.

Most of the art schools which train unsuspecting students for careers in advertising still subscribe to the mystique of the Bauhaus. They hold that the success of an advertisement depends on such things as "balance," "movement," and "design." But can they *prove* it?

My research suggests that these aesthetic intangibles do not increase sales, and I cannot conceal my hostility to the old school of art directors who take such preachments seriously. Imagine my horror when their college of cardinals, the august Art Directors Club, gave Henry Luce, Frank Stanton, Henry Ford and myself special awards for "encouraging art directors to work in the best possible climate." Did they not know that I wage war on art-directoritis, the disease which reduces advertising campaigns to impotence?

I no longer enter my agency's layouts in the contests organized by the art directors' societies, for fear that one of them might be disgraced by an award. Their gods are not my gods. I have my own dogma, and it springs from observing the behavior of human beings, as recorded by Dr. Gallup, Dr. Starch, and the mail-order experts.

Always design your layout for the publication in which it will appear, and never approve it until you have seen how it looks when pasted into that publication. The almost universal practice of appraising layouts *in vacuo*, mounted on gray cardboard and covered with cellophane, is dangerously misleading. A layout must relate to the graphic climate of the newspaper or magazine which is to carry it.

A young and inexperienced client recently said to me, "I knew which of your layouts was the best as soon as I saw them tacked up on my bulletin board." That is not the environment in which readers see advertisements.

There is no need for advertisements to *look* like advertisements. If you make them look like editorial pages, you will attract about 50 per cent more readers. You might think that the public would resent this trick, but there is no evidence to suggest that they do.

Our Zippo advertisements are laid out with the same kind of straightforward simplicity that the *Life* editors use. No gadgetry. No clutter. No arty use of type for purposes of decoration. No hand lettering. No trade marks. No symbols. (Trade marks and symbols were valuable in olden days, because they made it possible for illiterates to identify your brand. But illiteracy has disappeared in the United States, and you can now rely on printed names for purposes of identification.)

Magazine editors have discovered that people read the explanatory captions under photographs more than they read the text of articles; and the same thing is true of advertisements. When we analyzed Starch data on advertisements in *Life*, we found that on the average *twice* as many people read the captions as read the body copy. Thus captions offer you twice the audience you get for body copy. It follows that you should never use a photograph without putting a caption under it, and each caption should be a miniature advertisement, complete with brand name and promise.

If you can keep your body copy down to 170 words, you should set it in the form of a caption under your photograph, as we have done in our magazine advertisements for Tetley Tea.

If you need very long copy, there are several devices which are known to increase its readership:

(1) A display subhead of two or three lines, between your headline and your body copy, will heighten the reader's appetite for the feast to come.

(2) If you start your body copy with a large initial letter, you will increase readership by an average of 13 per cent.

(3) Keep your opening paragraph down to a maximum of eleven words. A long first paragraph frightens readers away. All your paragraphs should be as short as possible; long paragraphs are fatiguing.

(4) After two or three inches of copy, insert your first cross-head, and thereafter pepper cross-heads throughout. They keep the reader marching forward. Make some of them interrogative, to excite curiosity in the next run of copy. An ingenious sequence of boldly displayed cross-heads can deliver the substance of your entire pitch to glancers who are too lazy to wade through the text.

(5) Set your copy in columns not more than forty characters wide. Most people acquire their reading habits from newspapers, which use columns of about twenty-six characters. The wider the measure, the fewer the readers.

(6) Type smaller than 9-point is difficult for most people to read. This book is set in 10 point.

(7) Serif type like this is easier to read than **sans serif type** like this. The Bauhaus brigade is not aware of this fact.

(8) When I was a boy it was fashionable to make copywriters square up every paragraph. Since then it has been discovered that "widows" increase readership, except at the bottom of a column, where they make it too easy for the reader to quit.

(9) Break up the monotony of long copy by setting key paragraphs in boldface or italic.

(10) Insert illustrations from time to time.

(11) Help the reader into your paragraphs with arrowheads, bullets, asterisks, and marginal marks.

(12) If you have a lot of unrelated facts to recite, don't try to relate

them with cumbersome connectives; simply *number* them, as I am doing here.

(13) Never set your copy in reverse (white type on a black background), and never set it over a gray or colored tint. The old school of art directors believed that these devices *forced* people to read the copy; we now know that they make reading physically impossible.

(14) If you use leading between paragraphs, you increase readership by an average of 12 per cent.

The more typographical changes you make in your headline, the fewer people will read it. At our agency we run straight through our headlines in the same type face, in the same size, and in the same weight.

Set your headline, and indeed your whole advertisement, in lower case. CAPITAL LETTERS ARE MUCH HARDER TO READ, PROBABLY BECAUSE WE LEARN TO READ in lower case. People read all their books, newspapers, and magazines in lower case.

Never deface your illustration by printing your headline over it. Old-fashioned art directors love doing this, but it reduces the attention value of the advertisement by an average of 19 per cent. Newspaper editors never do it. In general, imitate the editors; they form the reading habits of your customers.

When your advertisement is to contain a coupon, and you want the maximum returns, put it at the top, bang in the middle. This position pulls 80 per cent more coupons than the traditional outside-bottom of the page. (Not one advertising man in a hundred knows this.)

H. L. Mencken once said that nobody ever went broke underestimating the taste of the American public. That is not true. I have come to believe that it pays to make all your layouts project a feeling of good taste, provided that you do it unobtrusively. An ugly layout suggests an ugly product. There are very few products which do not benefit from being given a First-Class ticket through life. In a socially mobile society, people do not like to be seen consuming products which their friends regard as Second-Class.

POSTERS

Not long ago I received a touching tribute to one of my posters, in the form of a letter from the pastor of an Ethiopian Baptist Church in California:

Dear Mr. Ogilvy:

I am the head of a small church group which is spreading the Lord's word on the highways of California. We use a lot of poster advertising and run into many problems due to high art costs. I saw the poster for Schweppes, *the one with the bearded man who has his arms stretched out* . . . What I would like to know is, can you send that photograph along to me when you are done with it? We would have JESUS SAVES printed on it, and put it up on the highways of California, spreading the Lord's word.

If my client's face could become identified with the Son of God, we would never have to spend another penny on advertising, and the whole Baptist world would be converted to Schweppes. My imagination boggled. Only fear of losing my commissions persuaded me to tell the pastor that Commander Whitehead was not worthy of this holy role.

I have never liked posters. The passing motorist does not have time to read more than six words on a poster, and my early experiences as a door-to-door salesman convinced me that it is impossible to sell anything with only six words. In a newspaper or magazine advertisement, I can use *hundreds* of words. Posters are for sloganeers.

As a private person, I have a passion for landscape, and I have never seen one which was improved by a billboard. Where every prospect pleases, man is at his vilest when he erects a billboard. When I retire from Madison Avenue, I am going to start a secret society of masked vigilantes who will travel about the world on silent motor bicycles, chopping down posters at the dark of the moon. How many juries will convict us when we are caught in these acts of beneficent citizenship?

The people who own the billboards are unscrupulous lobbyists. They have done their foul best to torpedo the legislation which prohibits posters on the new American turnpikes. They plead that the poster industry employs thousands of workers. So do brothels.

However, posters are still with us, and sooner or later you may be called upon to design one. So here goes.

Try to make your poster a *tour de force* – what Savignac calls a "visual scandal." If you overdo the scandal, you will stop the traffic and cause fatal accidents.

In Europe it has long been the fashion to criticize American posters for being so low-brow. Nobody could pretend that American posters can hold their own, esthetically, with the posters of Cassandre, Leupin, Savignac and McKnight Kauffer. But, alas, there is reason to believe that the corny American style makes its point faster, and is better remembered, than the more distinguished designs of European artists.

During the second German War, the Canadian Government engaged my old boss, Dr. George Gallup, to measure the relative efficiency of several recruiting posters. Dr. Gallup found that the posters which worked best with the most people were those which used realistic artwork or photographs. Abstract or symbolic designs did not communicate their message fast enough.

Your poster should deliver the selling promise of your product, not only in words, but also pictorially. Only a handful of advertising men have the genius to do this, and I am not one of them.

If your poster is aimed at passing motorists – you rascal, you – it must do its work in *five seconds* . . . Research has shown that it will communicate faster if you use strong, pure colors; don't paint with a dirty palette. Never use more than three elements in your design, and silhouette them against a white background.

Above all, use the largest possible type (sans-serif), and make your brand-name visible at a glance. It seldom is.

If you will follow these simple directions, you will produce posters which do their job. But I must warn you that you will not endear yourself to connoisseurs of contemporary art. Indeed, you may find yourself pilloried as a yahoo.

VIII   How to Make Good Television Commercials

"The few seconds of an advertising commercial," says Stanhope Shelton, "will fit into a pillbox two and one half inches in diameter. This tiny pillbox-full represents several weeks of concentrated effort on the part of thirty people. It can make the difference between profit and loss."

I have found that it is easier to double the selling power of a commercial than to double the audience of a program. This may come as news to the Hollywood hidalgos who produce the programs and look down their noses at us obscure copywriters who write the commercials.

The purpose of a commercial is not to *entertain* the viewer, but to *sell* him. Horace Schwerin reports that there is no correlation between people *liking* commercials and being *sold* by them.

But this does not mean that your commercials should be deliberately bad-mannered. On the contrary, there is reason to believe that it pays to make them human and friendly, if you can do so without being unctuous.

In the early days of television, I made the mistake of relying on *words* to do the selling; I had been accustomed to radio, where there are no pictures. I now know that in television you must make your *pictures* tell the story; what you *show* is more important than what you *say* ... Words and pictures must march together, reinforcing each other. The only function of the words is to explain what the pictures are showing.

Dr. Gallup reports that if you say something which you don't also illustrate, the viewer immediately forgets it. I conclude that if you don't show it, there is no point in saying it. Try running your commercial with the sound turned off; if it doesn't sell without sound, it is useless.

Most commercials befuddle the viewer by drowning him in logorrhea, a torrent of words. I advise you to restrict yourself to ninety words a minute.

It is true that you can deliver somewhat more selling points in a television commercial than in a printed advertisement, but the most effective commercials are built around only one or two points, simply stated. A hodgepodge of many points leaves the viewer unmoved. That is why commercials should never be created in committee. Compromise has no place in advertising. Whatever you do, *go the whole hog*.

When you advertise in magazines and newspapers, you must start by attracting the reader's attention. But in television the viewer is already attending; your problem is not to frighten her away. It is fatal to warn her that she is about to hear "a friendly word from our sponsor." Her bladder will react to this stimulus as Pavlov's dog reacted to the sound of a bell: she will leave the room.

The purpose of most commercials is to deliver your selling promise in a way the viewer will remember next time she goes shopping. I therefore advise you to repeat your promise at least twice in every commercial, to illustrate it pictorially, and to print it on the screen as a "title" or "super."

The average consumer, poor dear, is now subjected to 10,000 commercials a year. Make sure that she knows the name of the product being advertised in your commercial. Repeat it, *ad nauseam*, throughout.* Show it in at least one title. And show her the package which you want her to recognize in the store.

Make your product the hero of the commercial, as it is the hero of our famous commercial for Maxwell House Coffee – just a coffeepot and a cup of coffee – "good to the last drop." (I did not invent this slogan; Theodore Roosevelt did.)

In television advertising you have exactly fifty-eight seconds to make your sale, and your client is paying $500 a second. Don't mess about with irrelevant lead-ins. Start selling in your first frame, and never stop selling until the last.

For products which lend themselves to selling by demonstration – e.g., cooking ingredients, make-up, and sinus remedies – television is the most powerful advertising medium ever invented. Success in using it depends more than anything else on your ingenuity in devising *believable* demonstrations. The publicity which has attended some of the Federal Trade Commission's indictments has made the American public suspicious of trickery.

Dr. Gallup is a fountain of useful information on how people react to different kinds of commercials. He tells us that commercials which start by setting up a problem, then wheel up your product

---

* One of my sisters has suggested that the name of our agency should be changed to Ad Nauseam, Inc.

to solve the problem, then prove the solution by demonstration, sell four times as many people as commercials which merely preach about the product.

Dr. Gallup also reports that commercials with a strong element of *news* are particularly effective. So you should squeeze every drop of news value out of the material available for your commercials.

But sometimes, alas, there *isn't* any news. Your product may have been on the market for generations, and there may have been no significant improvement in its formula. Some products cannot be presented as the solution to any problem. Some do not lend themselves to demonstration. What do you do when these surefire gambits are denied to you? Do you give up? Not necessarily. There is another gambit available which can move mountains: *emotion and mood.* It is a difficult gambit to use without inducing derision in the viewer, but it has been used with consummate success in Europe, notably by Mather & Crowther in their commercials for Player's Cigarettes.

The average consumer now sees 900 commercials a month, and most of them slide off her memory like water off a duck's back. For this reason you should give your commercials a touch of singularity, a burr that will make them stick in the viewer's mind. But be very careful how you do this; the viewer is apt to remember your burr but forget your selling promise.

At two o'clock one morning I awoke from a troubled sleep with such a burr in my mind, and wrote it down: open the Pepperidge Farm commercials by having Titus Moody drive a baker's wagon with a team of horses along a country lane. It worked.

Don't *sing* your selling message. Selling is a serious business. How would you react if you went into a Sears store to buy a frying pan and the salesman started singing jingles at you?

Candor compels me to admit that I have no conclusive research to support my view that jingles are less persuasive than the spoken word. It is based on the difficulty I always experience in hearing the words in jingles, and on my experience as a door-to-door salesman; I never sang to my prospects. The advertisers who believe in the selling power of jingles have never had to sell anything.

This prejudice of mine is not shared by all my partners. When I go on vacation they occasionally have time to foist a jingle on one of our clients, and at least one of their jingles made the welkin ring. This exception proves my rule.*

The screens in movie theaters are forty feet wide, which is big enough for crowd scenes and long-distance shots. But the television screen is less than two feet wide, which is not big enough for Ben Hur. I advise you to use nothing but extreme close-ups in television commercials.

Avoid hackneyed situations – delighted drinkers, ecstatic eaters, families exhibiting togetherness, and all the other clichés of poor old Madison Avenue. They do not increase the consumer's interest in buying your product.

---

* Since writing this paragraph, I have been shown research on two commercials for a famous brand of margarine. The commercials were identical, except that in one the words were spoken, while in the other they were sung. The spoken version switched three times as many consumers as the sung version.

IX How to Make Good Campaigns for Food Products, Tourist Destinations and Proprietary Medicines

MOST of the commandments in this book, and the research from which they derive, have to do with advertising in *general* . . . But every category of product presents its own special problems. When you advertise detergents, for example, you have to decide whether to promise that your product will wash whiter, or cleaner, or brighter. When you advertise whiskey, you have to decide how much prominence to give to the bottle. When you advertise deodorants, you have to decide how much emphasis to give to deodorizing your customer, and how much to keeping her dry.

Food Products

The advertising of food products presents many special problems. How, for example, can you make food look appetizing on a television screen? Can any combination of *words* persuade the reader of your advertisement that a food product *tastes* good? How important are promises of *nutrition*? Should you show people *eating* the product?

I have tried to answer such questions by research. What I have so far learned can be boiled down to twenty-two commandments:

Print

(1) Build your advertisement around *appetite* appeal.

(2) The larger your food illustration, the more appetite appeal.

(3) Don't show people in food advertisements. They take up space that is better devoted to the food itself.

(4) Use color. Food looks more appetizing in color than in black-and-white.

(5) Use photographs – they have more appetite appeal than artwork.

(6) One photograph is better than two or more. If you *have* to use several photographs, make one of them dominant.

(7) Give a *recipe* whenever you can. The housewife is always on the lookout for new ways to please her family.

(8) Don't bury your recipe in your body copy. Isolate it loud and clear.

(9) Illustrate your recipe in your main photograph.

(10) Don't print your recipe over a screen; it will be read by far more women if you print it on clean white paper.

(11) Get *news* into your advertisements whenever you can – news about a new product, an improvement in an old product, or a new use for an old product.

(12) Make your headline specific, rather than general.

(13) Include your *brand name* in your headline.

(14) Locate your headline and copy *below* your illustration.

(15) Display your package prominently, but don't allow it to dominate your appetite photograph.

(16) Be serious. Don't use humor or fantasy. Don't be clever in your headline. Feeding her family is a serious business for most housewives.

Television

(17) Show how to *prepare* your product.

(18) Use the problem-solution gambit whenever you can do so without being farfetched.

(19) Whenever possible, give *news* – and play it loud and clear.

(20) Show your product *early* in the commercial.

(21) Don't use sound for its own sake. Only use sound effects which are relevant to your product – the perking of a coffeepot, the sizzle of a steak, the crunch of cornflakes.

(22) Commercials are for selling. Don't allow *entertainment* to dominate.

Tourist Destinations

Experience as the advertising agent for the British Travel & Holidays Association, for Puerto Rico, and for the United States Travel Service has led me to certain conclusions as to what makes for good tourism advertising. They may be summarized as follows:

(1) Destination advertising is bound to affect the image of the country concerned. It is politically important that it should affect it *favorably* . . . If you run crummy advertisements for your country, you will make people think that it is a crummy country.

(2) Tourists do not travel thousands of miles to see things which they can see next door. For example, people who live in Switzerland cannot be persuaded to travel five thousand miles to see the mountains in Colorado. Advertise what is *unique* in your country.

(3) Your advertisements should establish in the reader's mind an image which she will never *forget*. The period of gestation between exposure to an advertisement and the purchase of a ticket is likely to be very long.

(4) Your advertisements appear in media which are read by people who can afford to travel long distances. These people are well educated. Do not insult their intelligence; write in adult language – not in the clichés of conventional travel advertising.

(5) The biggest barrier to international travel is cost. Your advertisements should help the reader to rationalize the cost of his journey by selling its cultural and status overtones.

(6) Patterns of travel are peculiarly subject to *fashion*. Your advertisements should put your country on the map as the place where "everybody" is going. Bandwagons work like magic in tourism.

(7) People *dream* about far-away places. Your advertisements should convert their dreams into action – transforming potential energy into kinetic energy. This can best be done by offering the reader specific how-to-do-it information. A combination of mouth-watering photographs and specific information has brought the best results for British, American and Puerto Rican tourism.

(8) Beware of esoteric subjects. They may interest the nationals of the country sponsoring the campaign, but the foreign tourist – the customer – is out to collect clichés.

My "Come To Britain" advertisements have been conspicuously successful, but they have been subjected to a drumfire of criticism in the British press. The charge against them is that they damage British prestige by projecting an antique image – too many thatched cottages, too much pomp and circumstance. I am rebuked for creating the impression that England is a bucolic little kingdom living on the glories of an ancient past. Why don't I show England "as she really is," the vital, industrialized, welfare state which has given the world penicillin, jet engines, Henry Moore and atomic-power stations?

While this kind of thing might well be *politically* valuable, the only purpose of our campaign is to attract tourists, and no American is going to cross the briny ocean to look at a power station. He would rather see Westminster Abbey; so would I.

When deciding which countries to visit when he goes abroad, the American tourist is influenced by his attitude to the local inhabitants. My surveys show that he expects the British to be polite, cultured, honest, straightforward, clean and moral. But he also expects them to be aloof, pompous and doleful. So, in our advertising, we do our best to correct the disagreeable aspects of this stereotype by writing about the *friendliness* of English people.

I have been surprised to find that American tourists do not "travel on their stomachs." As the graduate of a French kitchen, I find it difficult to believe that so many American tourists actually like English cooking better than French cooking, but such is the case. They cannot read French menus, and they detest rich sauces.

Nor is England at any disadvantage vis-à-vis the French when it comes to quenching the thirst of the American tourist. He may not appreciate English beer, but he would rather drink Scotch whisky than claret – a preference which is shared by an increasing number of Frenchmen. We live in terrible times.

I once found myself conspiring with a British cabinet minister as to how we might persuade Her Majesty's Treasury to cough up more money for the British travel advertising in America. Said he, "Why does any American in his senses spend his vacation in the cold damp of an English summer when he could equally well bask under Italian skies? I can only suppose that your advertising is the answer . . ."

Damn right.

Proprietary Medicines

Advertising drugs is a special art. Here, stated with the dogmatism of brevity, are the principles I recommend to those who practice this art: *

(1) A good patent-medicine advertisement seizes upon "the compelling difference" between your brand and its competitors.

(2) A good patent-medicine advertisement contains *news*. The news may be a new product, a new aspect of an existing product, a new diagnosis, or a new name for a familiar complaint – like halitosis.

(3) A good patent-medicine advertisement has a feeling of *seriousness*. Physical discomfort is no joking matter to the sufferer. He welcomes recognition of the reality of his complaint.

(4) A good patent-medicine advertisement conveys a feeling of *authority*. There is a doctor-patient relationship inherent in medicine copy, not merely a seller-buyer relationship.

(5) The advertisement should not merely extol the merits of your product; it should also *explain the disease* . . . The sufferer should feel that he has learned something about his condition.

(6) Do not strain credulity. A person in pain wants to believe that you can help him. His will to believe is an active ingredient in the efficacy of the product.

* I have to thank Louis Redmond for help in arriving at these principles.

X How to Rise to the Top of the Tree (Advice to the Young)

One of my Irish ancestors entered the service of John Company and succeeded in "shaking the Pagoda-tree." In other words, he made a fortune. Now I am an ancestor myself, and I spend my waking hours shaking the Pagoda-tree on Madison Avenue. How is it done?

After watching the careermanship of my own employees for fourteen years, I have identified a pattern of behavior which leads rapidly to the top.

First, you must be ambitious, but you must not be so nakedly aggressive that your fellow workers rise up and destroy you. *Tout soldat porte dans sa giberne le bâton de maréchal*... Yes, but don't let it stick out.

If you go straight into an advertising agency after leaving the Harvard Business School, conceal your arrogance and keep up your studies. After a year of tedious training, you will probably be made an assistant account executive – a sort of midshipman. The moment that happens, set yourself to becoming the best-informed man in the agency on the account to which you are assigned. If, for example, it is a gasoline account, read text books on the chemistry, geology and distribution of petroleum products. Read all the trade journals in the field. Read all the research reports and marketing plans that your agency has ever written on the product.

Spend Saturday mornings in service stations, pumping gasoline and talking to motorists. Visit your client's refineries and research laboratories. Study the advertising of his competitors. At the end of your second year, you will know more about gasoline than your boss; you will then be ready to succeed him.

Most of the young men in agencies are too lazy to do this kind of homework. They remain permanently superficial.

Claude Hopkins attributed his success to the fact that he worked twice as long hours as other copywriters, and thus made his way up the ladder at twice their speed. One of the best agencies born in the last forty years owes its supremacy to the fact that its founder was so unhappy with his wife that he rarely left the office before midnight. In my bachelor days I used to work until the small hours. If you prefer to spend all your spare time growing roses or playing with your children, I like you better, but do not complain that you are not being promoted fast enough. Managers promote the men who produce the most.

If people in advertising agencies were paid on a piece-work basis, the drones would get their just deserts and the dynamos would triumph even faster than they do now. When Dr. William B. Shockley studied the creativity of scientists in the Bell Laboratories, he discovered that those in the most creative quartile applied for *ten times* as many patents as those in the least creative quartile, but were paid only 50 per cent more. Unfair? Yes, I think so. Albert Lasker used to pay the less productive copywriters at Lord & Thomas $100 a week, but he paid Claude Hopkins $50,000 for every $1,000,000 worth of advertising he wrote. A profitable time was had by all – Lasker, Hopkins and their clients.

Nowadays it is the fashion to pretend that no single individual is ever responsible for a successful advertising campaign. This emphasis on "team-work" is bunkum – a conspiracy of the mediocre majority. No advertisement, no commercial and no image can be created by a committee. Most top managements are secretly aware of this, and keep their eyes open for those rare individuals who lay golden eggs. These champions can no longer be rewarded on the Hopkins scale, but they are the only men in advertising agencies who are immune to the threat of dismissal in times of scarcity. They give value for money.

Most of the work you do in an agency will be routine maintenance. If you do it well, you will make gradual progress, but your golden opportunity will come when you rise to a great occasion. The trick is to recognize the great occasion when it presents itself.

Several years ago Lever Brothers asked their seven agencies to submit policy papers on the television medium, which was then quite new. The other agencies put in adequate papers of five or six pages, but a young man on my staff took the trouble to assemble every conceivable statistic and, after working day and night for three weeks, came up with an analysis which covered one hundred and seventy-seven pages. His lazy colleagues sneered at him as a "compulsive worker," but one year later he was elected to our board of directors. On such isolated incidents are most successful careers built. *Ii faut épater les clients.*

Most of the able young men who come into agencies nowadays are determined to become account executives, probably because they have been taught in business school that their mission in life is to manage and administer rather than to do specialist work. It escapes their attention that the heads of the six biggest agencies in the world were all *specialists* before they reached the top. Four of them were copywriters, one was in media and one in research. Not one of them had ever been an account executive.

It is much more difficult to make your mark as an account executive than as a specialist, because it is rare for an account executive to have an opportunity to cover himself with glory; almost all the spectacular triumphs are performed by the specialists. I would therefore advise my own son to specialize – in media, research or copy. He would find the competition less formidable in these departments, he would find more frequent opportunities to rise above routine maintenance work, and he would acquire an expertise which gives a man security – psychological and financial.

Perhaps some young men are attracted by the travel and entertainment which attach to the work of an account executive. They will quickly find that lunching in good restaurants is no fun if you have to explain a declining share-of-market while eating the soufflé; and riding the circuit of test markets can be a nightmare if one of your children is in the hospital.

If my son ignored my advice and became an account executive, I would offer him this advice:

(1) Sooner or later, a client will blackball you – either because he dislikes you, or because you have failed him, or because he attributes to you what is really the failure of some service department in your agency. When this happens to you, *don't be downhearted!* I know the head of an agency who survived being blackballed by three clients in one year.

(2) You can probably get by if you never function as more than a

mere channel of communication between your client and your service departments, like a waiter who shuttles between the chefs in the kitchen and the customers in the dining room. Such account executives are better called "contact men." No doubt you will perform this necessary function with aplomb, but I hope you will see your job in larger terms. Good account executives acquire the most complicated expertise of all: they become *marketers.*

(3) However hard you work, and however knowledgeable you become, you will be unable to represent your agency at the client's policy levels until you are at least thirty-five. One of my partners owes the rapidity of his ascent to the fact that he went bald when he was thirty, and another had the good fortune to become white-headed at forty. Be patient.

(4) You will never become a senior account executive unless you learn to make *good presentations* . . . Most of your clients will be large corporations, and you must be able to sell plans and campaigns to their committees. Good presentations must be well written, and well delivered. You can learn to write them well by studying the work of your masters, and by taking pains. You can learn to deliver them well by observing the techniques of the professionals – notably the Nielsen presenters.

(5) Do not make the common mistake of regarding your clients as hostile boobs. Make friends with them. Behave as if you were on their team. Buy shares in their company. Try not to become entangled in their politics; it would be a pity to lose an account because you backed the wrong horse. Emulate Talleyrand, who served France through seven regimes, and the Vicar of Bray – "Whatsoever king shall reign, I will be the Vicar of Bray, sir!"

(6) In your day-to-day negotiations with clients and colleagues, fight for the kings, queens and bishops, but throw away the pawns. A habit of graceful surrender on trivial issues will make you difficult to resist on those rare occasions when you must stand and fight on a major issue.

(7) Don't discuss your client's business in elevators, and keep their secret papers under lock and key. A reputation for leaking may ruin you.

(8) When you want to plant an idea in the mind of a copywriter or research director, do it privately and tactfully. The poacher is not popular on Madison Avenue.

(9) If you are brave about admitting your mistakes to your clients and your colleagues, you will earn their respect. Candor, objectivity and intellectual honesty are a *sine qua non* for the advertising careerist.

(10) Learn to write lucid interoffice memoranda. Remember that the senior people to whom they are addressed have more on their plates – and in their brief cases – than you do; the longer your memos, the less likely they are to be read by men who have the power to act on them. In 1941 Winston Churchill sent the following memo to the First Lord of the Admiralty:

> Pray state this day, *on one side of a sheet of paper*, how the Royal Navy is being adapted to meet the conditions of modern warfare. [Italics mine.]

Never forget that you are paid more than your contemporaries in other businesses and professions. There are three reasons for this.

First, the demand for able advertising men is greater than the supply. Second, the fringe benefits, while substantial, are less than you would receive in the Army or many manufacturing corporations. Third, there is less security of tenure in advertising than in most other jobs. Try your damnedest to keep your expenditure below your income, so that you can survive a period of unemployment. Take up the options you are given to buy stock in your agency. And invest in other directions. Social Security is mighty short commons for an advertising agent of sixty-five.

I have come to think that one of the most revealing signs of a young man's capacity is the use he makes of his vacations. Some fritter away those precious three weeks, while some get more out of them than all the rest of the year put together. I offer this recipe for refreshing vacations:

Don't stay at home and putter around the house. You need a change of scene.

Take your wife, but leave the children with a neighbor. Small fry are a pain in the neck on a vacation. Shut yourself off from exposure to advertising.

Take a sleeping pill every night for the first three nights. Get plenty of fresh air and exercise.

Read a book every day – twenty-one books in three weeks. (I assume that you have already taken the Book-of-the-Month Club's rapid reading course, and that you can do 1,000 words a minute.)

Broaden your horizons by going abroad, even if you have to

travel steerage. But don't travel so much that you come back
cross and exhausted.

The psychiatrists say that everybody should have a hobby. The
hobby I recommend is *advertising* . . . Pick a subject about which
your agency knows too little, and make yourself an authority on it.
Plan to write one good article every year, and place it in the
Harvard Business Review. Rewarding subjects: the psychology of
retail pricing, new ways to establish the optimum advertising
budget, the use of advertising by politicians, obstacles which
prevent international advertisers using the same campaigns all
over the world, the conflict between reach and frequency in media
planning. Once you become the acknowledged authority on any of
these troublesome subjects, you will be able to write your own
ticket.

In short, put your shoulder to the wheel, but be careful to pick the
right wheel. Says Sophie Tucker, "I've been rich and I've been
poor. Believe me, honey, rich is best."

XI Should Advertising Be Abolished?

Not long ago Lady Hendy, my Socialist elder sister, invited me to agree with her that advertising should be abolished. I found it difficult to deal with this menacing suggestion, because I am neither an economist nor a philosopher. But at least I was able to point out that opinion is divided on the question.

The late Aneurin Bevan thought that advertising was "an evil service." Arnold Toynbee (of Winchester and Balliol) "cannot think of any circumstances in which advertising would not be an evil." Professor Galbraith (Harvard) holds that advertising tempts people to squander money on "unneeded" possessions when they ought to be spending it on public works.

But it would be a mistake to assume that every liberal shares the Bevan-Toynbee-Galbraith view of advertising. President Franklin Roosevelt saw it in a different light:

> If I were starting life over again, I am inclined to think that I would go into the advertising business in preference to almost any other . . . The general raising of the standards of modern civilization among all groups of people during the past half century would have been impossible without the spreading of the knowledge of higher standards by means of advertising.

Sir Winston Churchill agrees with Mr. Roosevelt:

> Advertising nourishes the consuming power of men. It sets up
> before a man the goal of a better home, better clothing,
> better food for himself and his family. It spurs individual
> exertion and greater production.

Almost all serious economists, of whatever political color, agree
that advertising serves a useful purpose *when it is used to give information about new products*. Thus Anastas L. Mikoyan, the Russian:

> The task of our Soviet advertising is to give people exact
> information about the goods that are on sale, to help to
> create new demands, to cultivate new tastes and requirements,
> to promote the sale of new kinds of goods and to explain
> their uses to the consumer. The primary task of Soviet
> advertising is to give a truthful, exact, apt and striking
> description of the nature, quality and properties of the goods
> advertised.

The Victorian economist Alfred Marshall also approved of
"informative" advertising for new products, but condemned what
he called "combative" advertising as a waste. Walter Taplin of the
London School of Economics points out that Marshall's analysis of
advertising "shows indications of those prejudices and emotional
attitudes to advertising from which nobody seems to be completely
free, not even classical economists." There was, indeed, a streak of
prissiness in Marshall; his most illustrious student, Maynard
Keynes, once described him as "an utterly absurd person." What
Marshall wrote about advertising has been cribbed by many later
economists, and it has become orthodox doctrine to hold that
"combative" – or "persuasive" – advertising is economic waste. Is it?

My own clinical experience would suggest that the kind of informative factual advertising which the dons endorse is more effective, *in terms of sales results,* than the "combative" or "persuasive" advertising which they condemn. Commerical self-interest and academic virtue march together.

If all advertisers would give up flatulent puffery, and turn to the kind of factual, informative advertising which I have provided for Rolls-Royce, KLM Royal Dutch Airlines, and Shell, they would not only increase their sales, but they would also place themselves on the side of the angels. The more informative your advertising, the more persuasive it will be.

In a recent poll conducted among thought-leaders, Hill & Knowlton asked, "*Should advertisers give the facts and only the facts?*" The vote in favor of this austere proposition was strikingly affirmative:

	YES
Religious leaders	76%
Editors of highbrow publications	74
High school administrators	74
Economists	73
Sociologists	62
Government officials	45
Deans of colleges	33
Business leaders	23

Thus we see that factual advertising is very widely regarded as a Good Thing. But when it comes to "persuasive" advertising for one old brand against another, the majority of economists follow Marshall in condemning it. Rexford Tugwell, who earned my undying admiration for inspiring the economic renaissance of

Puerto Rico, condemns the "enormous waste involved in the effort
to turn trade from one firm to another." The same dogma comes
from Stuart Chase:

> Advertising makes people stop buying Mogg's soap, and start
> buying Bogg's soap . . . Nine-tenths and more of advertising is
> largely competitive wrangling as to the relative merits of two
> undistinguished and often undistinguishable compounds . . .

Pigou, Braithwaite, Baster, Warne, Fairchild, Morgan, Boulding,
and other economists say essentially the same thing, many of them
in almost the same words, except that they leave Mogg & Bogg to
Stuart Chase, substituting Eureka & Excelsior, Tweedledum &
Tweedledee, Bumpo & Bango. Read one of them, and you have
read them all.

I will let these dons in on a curious secret. The combative-persua-
sive kind of advertising which they condemn is not nearly as *profitable* as the informative kind of advertising which they approve.

My experience has been that it is relatively easy for advertising to
persuade consumers to try a *new* product. But they grow madden-
ingly deaf to the advertising of products which have been around
for a long time.

Thus we advertising agents get more mileage out of advertising
new products than old ones. Once again, academic virtue and
commercial self-interest march together.

Does advertising raise prices? There has been too much sloppy argument on both sides of this intricate question. Few serious studies
have been made of the effect of advertising on prices. However,

Professor Neil Borden of Harvard has examined hundreds of case histories. With the aid of an advisory committee of five other formidable professors, he reached conclusions which should be more widely studied by other dons before they pop off on the economics of advertising. For example, "In many industries the large scale of operations made possible in part through advertising has resulted in reductions in manufacturing costs." And, "the building of the market by means of advertising and other promotional devices not only makes price reductions attractive or possible for large firms, it also creates an opportunity to develop private brands, which generally are offered at lower prices." Indeed they are; when I am dead and opened, you shall find not "Calais" lying in my heart, as Mary Tudor prophesied would be found in hers, but "Private Brands." They are the natural enemies of us advertising agents. Twenty per cent of total grocery sales are now private brands, owned by retailers and not advertised. Bloody parasites.

Professor Borden and his advisers reached the conclusion that advertising, "though certainly not free from criticism, is an economic asset and not a liability."* Thus did they agree with Churchill and Roosevelt. However, they did not support all the shibboleths of Madison Avenue. They found, for example, that advertising does not give consumers sufficient information. My experience at the working level leads me to agree.

It is worth listening to what the men who pay out huge sums of their stockholders' money for advertising say about its effect on prices. Here is Lord Heyworth, the former head of Unilever:

* *The Economics of Advertising*, Richard D. Irwin (Chicago, 1942) pages xxv-xxxix.

Advertising . . . brings savings in its wake. On the distribution
side it speeds up the turnover of stock and thus makes lower
retail margins possible, without reducing the shopkeeper's
income. On the manufacturing side it is one of the factors
that make large scale production possible and who would
deny that large scale production leads to lower costs?

Essentially the same thing has recently been said by Howard
Morgens, the President of Procter & Gamble:

Time and again in our company, we have seen the start of
advertising on a new type of product result in savings that are
considerably greater than the entire advertising cost . . . The
use of advertising clearly results in lower prices to the public.

In most industries the cost of advertising represents less than 3 per
cent of the price consumers pay at retail. But if advertising were
abolished, you would lose on the swings much of what you saved
on the roundabouts. For example, you would have to pay a fortune
for the Sunday *New York Times* if it carried no advertising. And just
think how dull it would be. Jefferson read only one newspaper,
"and that more for its advertisements than its news." Most housewives would say the same.

Does advertising encourage monopoly? Professor Borden found that
"in some industries advertising has contributed to concentration
of demand and hence has been a factor in bringing about concentration of supply in the hands of a few dominant firms." But he
concluded that advertising is not a *basic cause* of monopoly. Other
economists have proclaimed that advertising contributes to
monopoly. I agree with them. It is becoming progressively more
difficult for small companies to launch new brands. The entrance

fee, in terms of advertising, is now so large that only the entrenched giants, with their vast war chests, can afford it. If you don't believe me, try launching a new brand of detergent with a war chest of less than $10,000,000.

Furthermore, the giant advertisers are able to buy space and time far more cheaply than their little competitors, because the media owners cosset them with quantity discounts. These discounts encourage big advertisers to buy up little ones; they can do the same advertising at 25-per-cent less cost, and pocket the saving.

Does advertising corrupt editors? Yes it does, but fewer editors than you may suppose. The publisher of a magazine once complained to me, in righteous indignation, that he had given one of my clients five pages of editorial and had received in return only two pages of advertising. But the vast majority of editors are incorruptible.

Harold Ross resented advertising, and once suggested to his publisher that all advertisements in *The New Yorker* should be put on one page. His successor exhibits the same sort of town-and-gown snobbery, and loses no opportunity to belittle what he calls "ad-men." Not long ago he published a facetious attack on two of my campaigns, sublimely indifferent to the fact I have filled 1,173 pages of his magazine with uncommonly ornamental advertisements. It strikes me as bad manners for a magazine to accept one of my advertisements and then attack it editorially – like inviting a man to dinner and then spitting in his eye.

I have often been tempted to punish editors who insult my clients. When one of our advertisements for the British Industries Fair appeared in an issue of the *Chicago Tribune* which printed one of

Colonel McCormick's ugly diatribes against Britain, I itched to pull the campaign out of his paper. But to do so would have blown a gaping hole in our coverage of the Middle West, and might well have triggered a brouhaha about advertising pressure on editors.

Can advertising foist an inferior product on the consumer? Bitter experience has taught me that it cannot. On those rare occasions when I have advertised products which consumer tests found inferior to other products in the same field, the results have been disastrous. If I try hard enough, I can write an advertisement which will persuade consumers to buy an inferior product, *but only once* – and most of my clients depend on repeat purchases for their profit. Phineas T. Barnum was the first to observe that "you may advertise a spurious article and induce many people to buy it once, but they will gradually denounce you as an impostor." Alfred Politz and Howard Morgens believe that advertising can actually accelerate the demise of an inferior product. Says Morgens, "The quickest way to kill a brand that is off in quality is to promote it aggressively. People find out about its poor quality just that much more quickly."

He goes on to point out that advertising has come to play a significant part in product improvement:

> Research people, of course, are constantly searching for ways to improve the things we buy. But believe me, a great deal of prodding and pushing and suggestions for those improvements also comes from the advertising end of the business. That's bound to be, because the success of a company's advertising is closely tied up with the success of its product development activities.

. . . Advertising and scientific research have come to work hand-in-glove on a vast and amazingly productive scale. The direct beneficiary is the consumer, who enjoys an ever-widening selection of better products and services.

On more than one occasion I have been instrumental in persuading clients not to launch a new product until they could develop one which would be demonstrably superior to those already on the market. Advertising is also a force for sustaining standards of quality and service. Writes Sir Frederic Hooper of Schweppes:

> Advertising is a guarantee of quality. A firm which has spent a substantial sum advocating the merits of a product and accustoming the consumer to expect a standard that is both high and uniform, dare not later reduce the quality of its goods. Sometimes the public is gullible, but not to the extent of continuing to buy a patently inferior article.

When we started advertising KLM Royal Dutch Airlines as "punctual" and "reliable," their top management sent out an encyclical, reminding their operations staff to live up to the promise of our advertising.

It may be said that a good advertising agency represents the consumer's interest in the councils of industry.

Is advertising a pack of lies? No longer. Fear of becoming embroiled with the Federal Trade Commission, which tries its cases in the newspapers, is now so great that one of our clients recently warned me that if any of our commercials were ever cited by the FTC for dishonesty, he would immediately move his account to another agency. The lawyer at General Foods actually required that our copywriters *prove* that Open-Pit Barbecue Sauce has an "old-fashioned flavor" before he would allow us to make this innocuous claim in advertisements. The consumer is better protected than she knows.

I cannot always keep pace with the changing rules laid down by the various bodies that regulate advertising. The Canadian Government, for example, applies one set of rules to patent medicine advertising, and the United States Government a totally different set. Some American states prohibit the mention of price in whiskey advertisements, while others insist upon it; what is forbidden in one state is obligatory in another. I can only take refuge in the rule which has always governed my own output: never write an advertisement which you wouldn't want your own family to see.

Dorothy Sayers, who wrote advertisements before she wrote whodunits and Anglo-Catholic tracts, says: "Plain lies are dangerous. The only weapons left are the *suggestio falsi* and the *suppressio veri.*" I plead guilty to one act of *suggestio falsi* – what we on Madison Avenue call a "weasel." However, two years later a chemist rescued my conscience by discovering that what I had falsely suggested was actually true.

But I must confess that I am continuously guilty of *suppressio veri.* Surely it is asking too much to expect the advertiser to describe the shortcomings of his product? One must be forgiven for putting one's best foot forward.

Does advertising make people want to buy products they don't need? If you don't think people need deodorants, you are at liberty to criticize advertising for having persuaded 87 per cent of American women and 66 per cent of American men to use them. If you don't think people need beer, you are right to criticize advertising for having persuaded 58 per cent of the adult population to drink it. If you disapprove of social mobility, creature comforts, and foreign travel, you are right to blame advertising for encouraging such wickedness. If you dislike affluent society, you are right to blame advertising for inciting the masses to pursue it.

If you are this kind of Puritan, I cannot reason with you. I can only call you a psychic masochist. Like Archbishop Leighton, I pray, "Deliver me, O Lord, from the errors of wise men, yea, and of good men."

Dear old John Burns, the father of the Labor movement in England, used to say that the tragedy of the working class was the poverty of their desires. I make no apology for inciting the working class to desire less Spartan lives.

Should advertising be used in politics? I think not. In recent years it has become fashionable for political parties to employ advertising agencies. In 1952 my old friend Rosser Reeves advertised General Eisenhower as if he were a tube of toothpaste. He created fifty commercials in which the General was made to read out hand-lettered answers to a series of phony questions from imaginary citizens. Like this:

Citizen: Mr. Eisenhower, what about the high cost of living?

General: My wife Mamie worries about the same thing. I tell her it's our job to change that on November 4th.

Between takes the General was heard to say, "To think that an old soldier should come to this."

Whenever my agency is asked to advertise a politician or a political party, we refuse the invitation, for these reasons:

(1) The use of advertising to sell statesmen is the ultimate vulgarity.

(2) If we were to advertise a Democrat, we would be unfair to the Republicans on our staff; and vice versa.

However, I encourage my colleagues to do their political duty by working for one of the parties – as individuals. If a party or a candidate requires technical advertising services, such as the buying of network time to broadcast political rallies, he can employ expert volunteers, banded together in an *ad hoc* consortium.

Should advertising be used in good causes of a nonpolitical nature? We advertising agents derive modest satisfaction from the work we do for good causes. Just as surgeons devote much of their time to operating on paupers without remuneration, so we devote much of our time to creating campaigns for charity patients. For example, my agency created the first campaign for Radio Free Europe, and in recent years we have created campaigns for the American Cancer Society, the United States Committee for the United Nations, the Citizens Committee To Keep New York City Clean, and Lincoln Center for the Performing Arts. The professional services we have donated to these causes have cost us about $250,000, which is equivalent to our profit on $12,000,000 of billing.

In 1959 John D. Rockefeller III and Clarence Francis asked me to increase public awareness of Lincoln Center, which was then in the planning stage. A survey revealed that only 25 per cent of the adult population of New York had heard of Lincoln Center. When our campaign was concluded, one year later, 67 per cent had heard of Lincoln Center. When I presented the plans for this campaign, I said:

> The men who conceived Lincoln Center, and particularly the big foundations which have contributed to it, would be dismayed if the people of New York came to think of Lincoln Center as the preserve of the upper crust . . . It is, therefore, important to create the right image: Lincoln Center is for *all* the people.

A survey conducted at the conclusion of the campaign showed that this democratic objective had been fulfilled. Those interviewed were presented with statements, and asked which they agreed with. Here are their votes:

Probably most people living in New York and its suburbs will visit Lincoln Center at one time or another	76%
Lincoln Center is only for wealthier people	4%

Most campaigns for good causes are contributed by one volunteer agency, but in the case of Lincoln Center, BBDO, Young & Rubicam, and Benton & Bowles volunteered to work in harness with us – a remarkable and harmonious quartet. The television commercials were made by BBDO, and New York stations donated $600,000 worth of time to running them. The radio commercials were made by Benton & Bowles, and the radio stations donated

$100,000 worth of time to running them. The printed advertise-
ments were made by Young & Rubicam and ourselves; *Reader's
Digest, The New Yorker, Newsweek,* and *Cue* ran them free.

When we volunteered to take over the campaign to Keep New York
City Clean, the number of streets rated clean had already
increased from 56 per cent to 85 per cent. I concluded that those
still littering must form a hard core of irresponsible barbarians
who could not be reformed by amiable slogans like the previous
agency's "Cast Your Ballot Here for a Cleaner New York."

A poll revealed that the majority of New Yorkers were not aware
that they could be fined twenty-five dollars for littering. We therefore developed a *tough* campaign, warning litterbugs that they
would be hauled into court. At the same time we persuaded the
New York Sanitation Department to recruit a flying squad of
uniformed men to patrol the streets on motor scooters, in search
of offenders. The newspapers and magazines donated an unprece-
dented amount of free space to running our advertisements, and
in the first three months the New York television and radio stations
gave us 1,105 free commercials. After four months, 39,004
summonses had been handed out, and the magistrates did their
duty.

Is advertising a vulgar bore? C. A. R. Crosland thunders in *The New
Statesman* that advertising "is often vulgar, strident and offensive.
And it induces a definite cynicism and corruption in both practitioners and audience owing to the constant intermingling of truth
and lies."

This, I think, is now the gravamen of the charge against advertising
among educated people. Ludwig von Mises describes advertising

as "shrill, noisy, coarse, puffing." He blames the public, as not reacting to dignified advertising; I am more inclined to blame the advertisers and the agencies – including myself. I must confess that I am a poor judge of what will shock the public. Twice I have produced advertisements which seemed perfectly innocent to me, only to be excoriated for indecency. One was an advertisement for Lady Hathaway shirts, which showed a beautiful woman in velvet trousers, sitting astride a chair and smoking a long cigar. My other transgression was a television commercial in which we rolled Ban deodorant into the armpit of a Greek statue. In both cases the symbolism, which had escaped me, inflamed more prurient souls.

I am less offended by obscenity than by tasteless typography, banal photographs, clumsy copy, and cheap jingles. It is easy to skip these horrors when they appear in magazines and newspapers, but it is impossible to escape them on television. I am angered to the point of violence by the commercial interruption of programs. Are the men who own the television stations so greedy that they cannot resist such intrusive affronts to the dignity of man? They even interrupt the inauguration of Presidents and the coronation of monarchs.

As a practitioner, I know that television is the most potent advertising medium ever devised, and I make most of my living from it. But, as a private person, I would gladly pay for the privilege of watching it without commercial interruptions. Morally, I find myself between the rock and the hard place.

It is television advertising which has made Madison Avenue the arch-symbol of tasteless materialism. If governments do not soon set up machinery for the regulation of television, I fear that the majority of thoughtful men will come to agree with Toynbee that "the destiny of our Western civilization turns on the issue of our struggle with all that Madison Avenue stands for." I have a vested interest in the survival of Madison Avenue, and I doubt whether it can survive without drastic reform.

Hill & Knowlton report that the vast majority of thought-leaders now believe that advertising promotes values that are too materialistic. The danger to my bread-and-butter arises out of the fact that what thought-leaders think today, the majority of voters are likely to think tomorrow. No, my darling sister, advertising should not be abolished. But it must be reformed.

A Collection of Ogilvy – isms

I believe in the Scottish proverb, 'Hard work never killed a man', men die of boredom, psychological conflict and disease. They do not die of hard work.

It is important to admit your mistakes and to do so before you are charged with them.

Big ideas are usually simple ideas

Get rid of sad dogs who spread doom.

In the best establishments, promises are always kept, whatever it may cost in agony and overtime.

Change is our lifeblood.

Tell the truth, but make the truth fascinating.

People do not buy from bad-mannered liars.

Tolerate genius.

It is a mistake to use highfalutin language when you advertise to uneducated people. I once used the word OBSOLETE, in a headline, only to discover that 33% of housewives had no idea of what it meant. In another headline I used the word INEFFABLE, only to discover that I didn't know what it meant myself.

No manufacturer ever complained that his advertising was selling too much.

We prefer the discipline of knowledge to the anarchy of ignorance.

I admire people with gentle manners who treat other people as human beings.

Index

Index

Adventures in Advertising
(Young), 53
Aeschines, 118
Alanbrooke, Lord, 50
American Association of
Advertising Agencies, 110
American Cancer Society, 190
American Express Company,
89
American Telephone &
Telegraph Company, 102
Ampex, 63
Anchor Brewery, 121
Anderson, Sir Colin, 93
Anderson, Sherwood, *fn.*. 142
Armstrong Cork Company,
Inc., 67–69
Arrow Shirts, 145
Art Directors Club, 58, 150
Art of Plain Talk, The (Flesch),
142
Ascoli, Max, 79
"At Sixty Miles an Hour the
Loudest Noise in the New
Rolls-Royce comes from the
electric clock," 135–6
Audience Research Institute, 75

Austin, 139–40
Ayer & Son, Inc., N. W., 102

Babb, Jervis J. (Jerry), 91
Ban, 89
Banzhof, Max, 67
Barnum, Phineas T., 186
Barron, Dr. Frank, 44–5
Barton, Bruce, 68
Bates, Ted, 52
Batton, Barton, Durstine &
Osborn, 76, 81, 191
BBDO (Batton, Barton,
Durstine & Osborn), 76, 81,
191
Beerbohm, Sir Max, 30
Behrman, S. N., 30
Bell Telephone Laboratories,
Inc., 172
Benson Ltd., S. H., 55
Bentley, 137
Benton, William, 94
Benton & Bowles, Inc., 76, 191
Berenson, Bernard, 118
Bernays, Edward L., 58
Betty Crocker, 129
Bevan, Aneurin, 179

Bevan, Robert (Bobby), 55
Billings, Le Moyne, 61
Blake, William, 42
Book-of-the-Month Club, Inc.,
    119, 177
Borden, Neil, 183–4
Bourgignon, M., 34
Bowles, Chester, 56, 94
"Bray, Vicar of," 175
Bristol-Myers Company, 51, 105
British Industries Fair, 185
British Travel & Holidays
    Association, 66, 167
Bromo Seltzer, 60
Bronfman, Samuel (Sam), 58,
    95, 108
Burlingham, Charles C., 39
Burnett, Leo, 118–19
Burnett Company, Inc., Leo, 76
Burns, John, 189
Burns, Hendry S. M. (Max), 65
Byron, Lord, *fn.* 142

Cadillac, 140
California, University of,
    Institute of Personality
    Assessment, 44
Cambridge University,
Cavendish Laboratory at, 49
Camels, 52
Campbell, Roy, 46
Campbell Soup Company, 51,

101, 129, 130
Caples, John, 119, 143
Carlton Hotel (London), 37
Carlyle, Thomas, 68
Carnation Company, 141
Carnegie, Andrew, 49
Carnegie Hall (New York), 48
Carroll, Lewis, 29
Casals Festival (Puerto Rico),
    146
Casals, Pablo, 146
Cassandre, 157
"Cast Your Ballot Here for a
Cleaner New York," 192
Cavendish Laboratory,
Cambridge University, 49
Cecil, George, 102, 120, 143
Cellarmaster, Brother, 108–9
Chase Manhattan Bank, The,
    57
Chase, Stuart, 182
Chicago Tribune, 185
Chicago, University of, 47;
    Sociology Department, 141
Christ Church (Oxford), 30
Christian Brothers, The, 108–9
Chrysler, Walter P., 52
Churchill, Sir Winston, 50, 76,
    179, 183
Citizens Committee To Keep
    New York City Clean, 190,
    192

Clark-Hooper, 120
Cody School of English, Sherwin, 127
Colby College (Maine), 93
Colgate-Palmolive Company, 52, 105
"Come to Britain," 146, 168
Conan Doyle, Sir Arthur, 115
Cone, Fairfax, 119
Container Corporation of America, 147
Cox, Edwin (Ed), 119
"Creams Your Skin While You Wash," 122
Cripps, Sir Stafford, 55
Crocker, Dr. John, 140
Crosland, C. A. R., 192
Cue, 192
Cunningham, Knox, 30

Daily Mail, The (London), 72
Damrosch, Walter, 48
Daudet, Alphonse, 108
Deep Cleanser, 122
Demosthenes, 118
Denny, Sir Henry, 66
"Do You Make These Mistakes in English? ", 127
Donegal Society, 68
Doumer, Paul, 35
Dove, 89, 122–3, 135

Down and Out in Paris and London (Orwell), 37
Doyle Dane Bernbach Inc., 144
Duffy, Bernard C. (Ben), 81
Dyer, George L., 138

Economics of Advertising, The (Irwin), *fn.* 183
Economist, The (London), 66
Edsel, 73
Edward VII, King of England, 39
Edwards, Dr. Charles, 138
Eisenhower, Dwight D., 189–90
Eldridge, Clarence, 101, 110
Elizabeth II, Queen of England, 139
Emerson, Ralph Waldo, 68
Erwitt, Elliott, 146
Escoffier, Auguste, 37, 143
Esso, 129
Esty, William (Bill), 51
Ethiopian Baptist Church, 156

Fatt, Arthur, 73
Faulkner, William, *fn.*. 142
Federal Trade Commission, 161, 187
Felling, Keith, 30
Fetres (Scotland), 30
Flesch, Dr. Rudolph, 142
Ford, Henry, 54, 120

Ford Motor Company, 101
Francis, Clarence, 191
"Friendly word from our
    sponsor, A," 160

Gaibraith, John Kenneth, 146,
    179
Gallup, Dr. George, 30, 75, 97,
    120, 137, 140, 144, 148, 151,
    157, 160, 162
"Gauchet, Père," 108
General Foods Corporation,
    52, 101, 105, 106, 115, 188
Getchel, Sterling, 52, 127
Gibbon, Edward, 99
Gilbert, W. S., 54
Gladstone, William E., 35
Glass Container Manufacturers
    Institute, 104
"Gloster, Sir Anthony," 131
Good Luck Margarine, 137, 139
"Good to the last drop," 161
Gordon-Walker, Patrick, 30
Great Britain, 89, 168–9
Grey Advertising, Inc., 73
Greyhound Bus Lines, 73
Groton School
    (Massachusetts), 140
Guide Culinaire (Escoffier), 37
Guinness & Son, Inc., Arthur,
    75
Guinness Stout, 129

Hall, Dr. Calvin, 148
Hallmark Cards Inc., 103
Hallowell, Roger, 92
Handel, George Frederick, 48
Handelsblatt (D?sseldorf), 72
Harrod, Roy, 30
Hart, Max, 139
Hart, Schaffner & Marx, 138
Harvard Business Review, 178
Harvard Business School, 171
Hathaway Shirt Company, 88,
    89, 93, 106, 145, 193
Hauser, Philip, 141
Havergal, Henry, 30
Hemingway, Ernest, *fn..* 142
Hendy, Lady, 179, 194
Henry VIII, King of England,
    66
Henry, Patrick, 68
Hewitt, Anderson (Andy), 56–7
Heyworth, Lord, 183
Hill& Knowlton, Inc., 181, 194
Hooper, Sir Frederic, 96–7, 187
Hopkins, Claude C., 47, 93,
    124, 137, 143, 172, 173
Hormone Cream, Helena
    Rubinstein's, 133
Hotchkiss School
    (Connecticut), 140
Houghton, Arthur, 93, 112
Hummert, Frank, 47, 93
Huxley, Aldous, 142

Ideal Homes Exhibition (London), 64
Inglis, Lord Justice General, 30
Institute of Personality Assessment, University of California, 44
International Paper Company, 49, 89
Irwin, Richard D., *fn*.. 183
"It's such a comfort to take a bus and leave the driving to us," 73
Ivory Soap, 129

James, Henry, 67
Jefferson, Thomas, 184–5
Jetté, Ellerton, 89, 106, 145
John Company, 171
Johnson, Dr. Samuel, 121
Jones, John Paul, 69
Jordan, Ned, 140

Kaganovitch, Lazar M., 62
Kauffer, McKnight, 157
Kennedy, John E., 47
Kent, 65
Kenyon & Eckhardt, Inc., 104
Kerensky, Alexander F., 62
Keynes, Maynard, 180
Kipling, Rudyard, 131
KLM Royal Dutch Airlines, 61, 89, 124, 148, 181, 187
Konoff, Alexander, 62

Lady Hathaway Shirts, 193
La Farge, John, 57
Lamb, Charles, *fn*. 142
Lambert, Gerard B. (Jerry), 108, 114, 130
Lambert Pharmacal Company, 114
Lasker, Albert D., 47, 172
Leffingwell, Russell C., 57
Leighton, Archbishop, 189
Lenin, Nikolai, 62
Lennen & Newell, Inc., 61
Leupin, 157
Lever Brothers Company, 51, 91, 105, 112, 173
Leverhulme, Lord, 86
Life, 65, 152
Lincoln Center for the Performing Arts, 191
Listerine, 114, 130
Little, Edward (Ed), 52
Lloyd George, David, 30
London School of Economics, 180
"Look at All Three," 127
Lord & Thomas, 93, 172
Lorillard Company, P., 65
Luce, Henry, 150
Lydecker, Garret, 98

Mabane, Lord, 66
Macaulay, Thomas B., 99
Macleod, Ian, 30
MacManus, Theodore F., 140
Macpherson, Niall, 40
Majestic, Hotel (Paris), 33, 34, 37, 38, 49
Manchester Guardian, The, 72
Marquand, J. P., *fn.* 142
Marshall, Alfred, 180, 182
Mary, Queen of England, 183
Mather & Crowther, Ltd., 55, 162
Maxwell, Sir Alexander H., 66
Maxwell House Coffee, 89, 106, 161
McCann-Erickson, 76, 94
McCann, Harry, 94
McCormick, Joseph M., 186
McElroy, Neil, 56
McKinsey & Company, Inc., 110
Mencken, Henry L., 155
Menninger, Dr. William, 39
Messiah (Handel), 48
Meynell, Sir Francis, 55
Mikoyan, Anastas L., 180
Mises, Ludwig von, 192
Mommsen, Theodor, 99
"Moody, Titus," 162
Morgan & Company, J. P., 57
Morgens, Howard, 184, 186

Mortimer, Charles G. (Charlie), 115
Moscoso, Teadoro (Ted), 79–80, 93, 108
Mozart, Wolfgang Amadeus, 117
Mu?oz-Marin, Luis, 80
Murphy, William B. (Bev), 130
"My dear, nothing in this world is worth buying," 31

New Republic, The, 62
New Statesman, The, 192
New York Times, The, 74, 184
New York Philharmonic, 64–5
New York University, School of Retailing, 135, 138
New Yorker, The, 49, 185, 192
Newsweek, 192
Nielsen, A. C. (Art), 130
Nielsen Company, A. C., 176

Ogilvy, Benson & Mather, 36, *passim*
Ogilvy, Francis, 55
"Old-fashioned flavor," 188
Old Gold, 65
On Some South African Novelists (Campbell), 46
Open-Pit Barbecue Sauce, 188
Operation Bootstrap (Puerto Rico), 79, 138

Orwell, George, 37
Oxford University, 30, 48, 99

Paepcke, Walter, 147
Page, Arthur, 57, 102
Pavilion Restaurant (New
    York), 33
Pavlov, Ivan P., 160
"Penalty of Leadership, The,"
    140
Penn, Irving, 144
Pepperidge Farm, 89, 162
Pinkerton, Allan, 68–9
"Pirate King, Richard A,"
    54
Pitard, M., 34–38
Play of the Week, 65
Player's Cigarettes, 162
Plymouth, 52, 127
P & O–Orient Lines, 89, 93
Politz, Alfred, 186
Prentis, Henning, 69
"Priceless ingredient of every
product is the honor and
    integrity of its maker, The,"
    141
"Private Brands," 183
Proctor & Gamble, 56, 102,
    105, 184
Psychology of Imagination, The
    (Barron), 44–5
Puerto Rico, 79–80, 93, 108,
    138, 146, 167, 182
Punch, 56

Rachmaninoff, Sergei, 48
Radio Free Europe, 190
Rayon Manufacturers'
    Association, 78
Reader's Digest, 192
Redmond, Louis, *fn*. 170
Reed & Barton, 92
Reeves, Rosser, 58, 189
Resor, Stanley, 53, 81
Retailing, New York University
    School of, 135, 138
Reynolds Tobacco Company,
    R. J., 52
Rigby, Sir Hugh, 125
Rinso, 92, 140
Rinso Blue, 49
Rockefeller, John D., Jr., 49
Rockefeller, John D., III, 191
Rolleston, Sir Humphry, 54
Rolls-Royce, Inc., 64, 67, 75,
    88–9, 101, 123, 136, 137, 181
Roosevelt, Eleanor, 139
Roosevelt, Franklin D., 179,
    183
Roosevelt, Theodore, 161
Roper, Elmo, 80
Ross, Harold, 49, 185
Rowntree and Company, Ltd.,
    fn. 67

Royal Dutch Airlines, KLM, 61,
    89, 124, 148, 181, 187
Rubicam, Raymond, 94, 118,
    120, 140–3
Rubinstein, Helena, 60, 61, 94,
    112, 134, 150
Ruder, William, 69
Rudolph, Harold, 120, 145
Ruml, Beardsley, 80
Russell, A. S., 30
Rutherford, Lord, 49

Savignac, 157
Sayers, Dorothy, *fn.* 55, 188
Scherman, Harry, 119
Schlitz Brewing Company,
    Joseph, 137
Schwab, Victor 0. (Vic), 119,
    138
Schweppes USA, Ltd., 88, 89,
    93, 96–7, 155–6, 187
Schwerin, Horace, 159
Seagram Distillers Company,
    58, 95, 108–9
Seagrove, Gordon, 108
Sears, Roebuck and Company,
    82, 89, 120, 123, 139, 163
Sellar, Walter, 30
Shakespeare, William, 117
Shaw, Bernard, *fn.* 142
Shell Oil Company, 51, 64–5,
    89, 124, 138, 181

Shelton, Stanhope, 159
Shockley, Dr. William, 172
"Somewhere West of Laramie,"
    140
Sonnenberg, Benjamin (Ben),
    72
Soul?, Henri, 33
Spaght, Dr. Monroe (Monty),
    65
Squibb & Sons, E. R., 140–1
Stahl-Meyer, Inc., 64
Standard Oil Company of New
    Jersey, 60, 61, 65
Stanton, Frank, 150
Starch, Dr. Daniel, 120, 140,
    152
Stephenson, Sir William, 30
Steuben Glass, 89, 93, 112
Stowell, Esty, 76–7
Sunoco, 57
Susskind, David, 65
Sutherland, Graham, 94

Talleyrand-Perigord, Charles
    Maurice de, 175
Taplin, Walter, 180
1066 and All That (Sellar), 30
Tetley Tea Company, Inc., 89,
    152
Thompson Company, J. Walter,
    53, 57, 76, 81, 94
Tide, 91

Time, 140
Times Literary Supplement, 136
Titus, Horace, 60
Toynbee, Arnold, 179, 193
Trevelyan, George, 99
Trotsky, Leon, 62
Tucker, Sophie, 178
Tugwell, Rexford Guy, 181

United States Committee for
   the United Nations, 190
United States Travel Service,
   69–72, 167

Vim, 112
"Visit U.S.A.," 70–2
Volkswagen of America, Inc.,
   144

Wanamaker, John, 86
Webster, John, 108

Wedgwood, Hensleigh, 55
Wedgwood & Sons, Inc.,
   Josiah, 55
Wellington, Duke of, 42
"Which Twin Has The Toni?",
   147
White Devil, The (Webster),
   108
Whitehead, Commander, 93,
   150, 156
'Williams, Ted, 139
"Wimsey, Lord Peter" *(The Nine
   Tailors)*, *fn.* 55

Young, James Webb, 120, 139,
   143
Young, John Orr, 52–3
Young & Rubicam, Inc., 101,
   145, 191, 192

Zippo, 89, 151

David Ogilvy CBE

1911 – 1999